Two Views of the Siege of Vicksburg, 1863

Two Views of the Siege of Vicksburg, 1863

My Cave Life in Vicksburg
A Lady
(Mary Webster Loughborough)

A Soldier's Story of the Siege of Vicksburg
Osborn H. Oldroyd

LEONAUR

Two Views of the Siege of Vicksburg, 1863
My Cave Life in Vicksburg
by A Lady (Mary Webster Loughborough)
and
A Soldier's Story of the Siege of Vicksburg
by Osborn H. Oldroyd

First published under the titles
My Cave Life in Vicksburg
and
A Soldier's Story of the Siege of Vicksburg From the Diary of Osborn H. Oldroyd

FIRST EDITION

Leonaur is an imprint
of Oakpast Ltd

Copyright in this form © 2013 Oakpast Ltd

ISBN: 978-1-78282-120-5 (hardcover)
ISBN: 978-1-78282-121-2 (softcover)

http://www.leonaur.com

Contents

My Cave Life in Vicksburg

Contents

To One
Who, Though Absent, is Ever Present,
This Little Waif
Is Tenderly and Affectionately
Dedicated

CHAPTER 1

Our Party Set Out for Vicksburg

It has been said that the peasants of the Campagna, in their semi-annual visits to the Pontine marshes, arrive piping and dancing; but it is seldom they return in the same merry mood, the malaria fever being sure to affect them more or less. Although I did not leave Jackson on the night of the 15th piping and dancing, yet it was with a very happy heart and very little foreboding of evil that I set off with a party of friends for a pleasant visit to Vicksburg. Like the peasants, I returned more serious and with a dismal experience. How little do we know with what rapidity our feelings may change! We had been planning a visit to Vicksburg for some weeks, and anticipating pleasure in meeting our friends. How gladly, in a few days, we left it, with the explosions of bombs still sounding in our ears! How beautiful was this evening: the sun glowed and warmed into mellow tints over the rough forest trees; over the long moss that swung in slow and stately dignity, like old-time dancers, scorning the quick and tripping movements of the present day!

Glowing and warming over all, this evening sun, this mellow, pleasant light, breaking in warm tints over the rugged ground of the plantation, showed us the home scenes as we passed; the sober and motherly cows going home for the evening's milking through the long lanes between the fields, where the fences threw shadows across the road; making strange, weird figures of the young colts' shadows, lean and long-limbed and distorted; the mothers, tired of eating the grass that grew so profusely, were standing in quiet contentment, or drank from the clear runs of water. And so we passed on by the houses, where the planter sat on his veranda, listening to the voice of his daughter reading the latest paper, while round her fair head, like a halo, the lingering beams of the sun played.

And on to Black River, "Big Black," with its slow, sluggish tide! Dark, like the Stygian stream, it flowed in the mist of the evening, the twilight. And soon we see Vicksburg, classic ground forever in America. The Hudson must now yield the palm to the Father of "Waters. Our interest will centre around spots hallowed by the deeds of our countrymen. I had thought, during the first bombardment of Vicksburg, that the town must have been a ruin; yet very little damage has been done, though very few houses are without evidence of the first trial of metal. One, I saw, with a hole through the window; behind was one of corresponding size through the panel of the door, which happened to be open. The corner of the piano had been taken off, and on through the wall the shot passed; one, also, passed through another house, making a huge gap through the chimney. And yet the inhabitants live in their homes (those who have not lost some loved one) happy and contented, not knowing what moment the house may be rent over their heads by the explosion of a shell.

"Ah!" said I to a friend, "how is it possible you live here?"

"After one is accustomed to the change," she answered, we do not mind it; but "becoming accustomed, that is the trial."

I was reminded of the poor man in an infected district who was met by a traveller and asked, "How do you live here?" "Sir, we die," was the laconic reply. And this is becoming accustomed. I looked over this beautiful landscape, and in the distance plainly saw the Federal transports lying quietly at their anchorage. Was it a dream? Could I believe that over this smiling scene, in the bright April morning, the blight of civil warfare lay like a pall?—lay over the fearful homesteads—some, even now, jarred by the shock of former conflicts—lay by the hearthstones, making moan in many a bereaved heart looking forward with vague fears to the coming summer.

What soul in the land but has felt and witnessed this grief—this unavailing sorrow for the brave and untimely dead? I thought of the letter from the sorrowing one in Iowa, whose son, a prisoner, I had nursed, receiving with the last breath words for the distant, unconscious mother; of her sorrow in writing of him in his distant grave; of her pride in him, her only son. How many in the land could take her hand and weep over a mutual sorrow! And in the hospital wards, men, who still hold the name of Americans, together were talking of battles, prisoners, and captors, when each told the other of acts of bravery performed on hostile fields, and took out pictures of innocent babes, little children, and wives, to show each other, all feeling a sympathy and interest in the unknown faces. Verily, war is a species of passionate insanity.

While standing and thinking thus, the loud booming of the guns in the water batteries startled me, the smoke showing that it was the battery just below me, that opened, I was told, on what was thought to be a masked battery on the opposite shore. No reply was elicited, however; and on looking through the glass, we saw in the line of levee, between the river and the Federal canal, a spot where new earth seemed to have been thrown up, and branches of trees to have been laid quite regularly in one place. This was all. General Lee, however, had ordered the spot to be fired on, and the firing continued some little time.

Our ride that evening had been delightful. We sat long on the veranda in the pleasant air, with the soft melody and rich swell of music from the band floating around us, while ever and *anon* my eye sought the bend of the river, two miles beyond, where the Federal transports, brought out in bold relief by the waning, crimson light of the evening, lay in seeming quiet. Still, resting in Vicksburg seemed like resting near a volcano.

CHAPTER 2

At Night the Signal Gun Sounds

At night I was sleeping profoundly, when the deep boom of the signal cannon startled and awoke me. Another followed, and I sprang from my bed, drew on my slippers and robe, and went out on the veranda. Our friends were already there. The river was illuminated by large fires on the bank, and we could discern plainly the huge, black masses floating down with the current, now and then belching forth fire from their sides, followed by the loud report, and we could hear the shells exploding in the upper part of town. The night was one of pitchy darkness; and as they neared the glare thrown upon the river from the large fires, the gunboats could be plainly seen. Each one, on passing the track of the brilliant light on the water, became a target for the land batteries. We could hear the gallop, in the darkness, of couriers upon the paved streets; we could hear the voices of the soldiers on the riverside.

The rapid firing from the boats, the roar of the Confederate batteries, and, above all, the screaming, booming sound of the shells, as they exploded in the air and around the city, made at once a new and fearful scene to me. The boats were rapidly nearing the lower batteries, and the shells were beginning to fly unpleasantly near. My heart beat quickly as the flashes of light from the portholes seemed facing us. Some of the gentlemen urged the ladies to go down into the cave at the back of the house, and insisted on my going, if alone. While I hesitated, fearing to remain, yet wishing still to witness the termination of the engagement, a shell exploded near the side of the house. Fear instantly decided me, and I ran, guided by one of the ladies, who pointed down the steep slope of the hill, and left me to run back for a shawl.

While I was considering the best way of descending the hill, another shell exploded near the, foot, and, ceasing to hesitate, I flew down, half sliding and running. Before I had reached the mouth of the cave, two more exploded on the side of the hill near me. Breathless and terrified, I found the entrance and ran in, having left one of my slippers on the hillside.

I found two or three of our friends had already sought refuge under the earth; and we had not been there long before we were joined by the remainder of the party, who reported the boats opposite the house. As I had again become perfectly calm and collected, I was sorry to find myself slightly fluttered and in a state of rapid heart-beatings, as shell after shell fell in the valley below us, exploding with a loud, rumbling noise, perfectly deafening. The cave was an excavation in the earth the size of a large room, high enough for the tallest person to stand perfectly erect, provided with comfortable seats, and altogether quite a large and habitable abode (compared with some of the caves in the city), were it not for the dampness and the constant contact with the soft earthy walls. We had remained but a short time, when one of the gentlemen came down to tell us that all danger was over, and that we might witness a beautiful sight by going upon the hill, as one of the transports had been fired by a shell, and was slowly floating down as it burned.

We returned to the house, and from the veranda looked on the burning boat, the only one, so far as we could ascertain, that had been injured, the other boats having all passed successfully by the city. We remained on the veranda an hour or more, the gentlemen speculating on the result of the successful run by the batteries. All were astonished and chagrined. It was found that very few of the Confederate guns had been discharged at all. Several reasons had been assigned; the real one was supposed to have been the quality of the fuses that were recently sent from Richmond, and had not been tried since their arrival. This night of all others they were found to be defective. The lurid glare from the burning boat fell in red and amber light upon the house, the veranda, and the animated faces turned toward the river—lighting the white magnolias, paling the pink crape myrtles, and bringing out in bright distinctness the railing of the terrace, where drooped in fragrant wreaths the clustering passion vine: fair and beautiful, but false, the crimson, wavering light.

I sat and gazed upon the burning wreck of what an hour ago had thronged with human life; with men whose mothers had this very night prayed for them; with men, whose wives tearfully hovered over little beds, kissing each tender, sleeping lid for the absent one. Had this night made them orphans? Did this smooth, deceitful current of the glowing waters glide over forms loved and lost to the faithful ones at home? O mother and wife! ye will pray and smile on, until the terrible tidings come: "Lost at Vicksburg!" Lost at Vicksburg! In how many a heart the name for years will lie like a brand!—lie until the warm heart and tried soul shall be at peace forever.

CHAPTER 3

Masked Battery on the Opposite Shore

At breakfast, on the morning of the 17th, we heard discussed the question, "Whether there was a masked battery on the opposite shore or not? After some words on the subject, *pro* and *con*, we ranged the shore with the glass, seeing what the gentlemen believed to be a battery. They had been talking some moments, when I took the glass and saw a number of Federal soldiers walking on the levee toward the spot where the battery was supposed to be. Several others seemed to be engaged on this very place removing the branches. I called one of the gentlemen to look. I had given up the glass but a few moments, when a volume of smoke burst from the embankment, and two shells were sent, one after the other, exploding at the depot just below us. It was indeed a battery, with two guns, which commenced playing on the city vigorously.

We were to leave that morning, and hearing that the cars would not venture up to the depot, went to a point below, where we found many anxious persons awaiting their arrival. We entered the cars, and were sitting quite securely and comfortably, when it was whispered around, much to the consternation of passengers, that they were ordered to approach the depot as near as possible, and take on freight; and thus we were carried up, under shelter of a high bluff, with many misgivings on my part, as shell after shell exploded on the hill above us. A nervous gentleman leaned forward and told me that we were in great danger, and, speaking in the same manner to many of the ladies, suggested that, if we made the request, the conductor would doubtless back into a safe place.

Although so frightened, his mode of relief was so evidently selfish that the gentlemen began joking him most unmercifully. In looking out of the window, although I felt a sympathy for the poor fellow, I could not but be amused at the ludicrous scene that presented itself: the porters bringing the baggage and small freight from the depot acted as if wild—now halting to await the course of a shell—then dashing forward, determined to reach the cars before another came. Two negroes were coming with a small trunk between them, and a carpet bag or two, evidently trying to show others of the profession how careless of danger they were, and how foolish "niggars" were to run "dat sort o' way."

A shell came ricocheting through the air and fell a few yards beyond the braves, when, lo! the trunk was sent tumbling, and landed bottom upward; the carpet bag followed—one grand somerset; and amid the cloud of dust that arose, I discovered one porter doubled up by the side of the trunk, and the other crouching close by a pile of plank. A shout from the negroes on the cars, and much laughter, brought them on their feet, brushing their knees and giggling, yet looking quite foolish, feeling their former prestige gone. Yet gentlemen and servants avoided the depot as much as possible; and whenever a portion of earth was seen to arise in a small volume, accompanied by smoke, men of both colours immediately ran (without casting a look behind) swiftly in the opposite direction, "gentlemen of colour" generally, in their haste, stumbling and turning one or two somersets before reaching a place of safety.

And so the shell continued coming, exploding on all sides, yet not happening to reach us. Soon the glad sound of the whistle was heard, and, after our long suspense, we felt the motion of the cars again, and were glad to leave Vicksburg, with the sound of the cannon and noise of the shell still ringing in our ears. Some young lady friends of mine were laughing and telling me of their experience during the danger of the previous night; of the fright and trouble they were in at the time the gunboats passed. Major Watts, of the Confederate Army, had given a very large party, which they attended; one dressed in a corn-coloured silk trimmed with black lace; another in blue silk trimmed with white point, and still another in white lace. In the confusion and alarm, as the first shell fell, one of the young girls, who was dancing with a brigadier-general, clasped her hands and exclaimed, "Where shall we go?"

In jest he said, "To the country for safety." Believing him serious, in the confusion that ensued, she told her young friends. They set out alone with all speed, frightened and trembling. Fortunately a gentleman friend, discovering their absence, overtook, and proceeded with them. As a shell would be heard coming, he would cry, "Fall!" and down they would drop in the dust, party dresses and all, lying until the explosion took place; then up, with wild eyes and fiercely beating hearts, flying with all speed onward. After running about a mile in the fewest moments possible, and falling several times, they stopped at the first house, and remained until their friends sent out for them in carriages.

"If you could have seen our party dresses when we reached home, and our hair, and the flowers, full of dust, you would never have forgotten us," cried one. "Ah!" said another, "we laugh gayly this morning, for we are leaving the guns behind us; but last night it was a serious business, and we absolutely ran for our lives."

How delighted I was with the quiet rest of our home in Jackson! I mentally forswore Vicksburg during the war. But *man proposes, and God disposes.*"

CHAPTER 4

Jackson Threatened

Our quiet was destined to be of short duration. We were startled one morning by hearing that Colonel Grierson, of the Federal Army, was advancing on Jackson. The citizens applied to General Pemberton to protect them. He answered that there was no danger. Suddenly, the ladies' carriage and saddle horses were pressed, and the clerks and young men of the town were mounted on them, and started out to protect us (!). I was told that the first time they met the Federal troops most of them were captured, and we heard of them no more. We need not have feared, for Colonel Grierson was spoken of everywhere (so some ladies from the district through which he passed, afterward told me) as a gentleman who would not allow his men to treat anyone with the slightest disrespect, or take the least article from a citizen's house; and they all treated ladies courteously. There was not one instance of unkindness to any human being, so far as I could learn. He should have the thanks of every brave man and Southern woman. This man, though an avowed enemy, scorned to torture or wage war on God's weaker creation.

Again the rumour came that from Canton a large Federal force was advancing on Jackson. Jackson was to be defended!! which I doubted. Soon General Pemberton left and went to Vicksburg—Mrs. Pemberton to Mobile. Batteries were being erected in different parts of the town—one directly opposite the house I was in. I stood considering one morning where it was best to go, and what it was best to do, when a quick gallop sounded on the drive, and a friend rode hastily up and said, "Are you going to leave?"

"Yes," I answered, "but I have not yet decided where to go."

"Well, I assure you there is no time for deliberation; I shall take my family to Vicksburg, as the safest place, and, if you will place yourself under my charge, I will see you safely to your husband."

So the matter was agreed upon, and we were to leave that evening. Still, I was in doubt; the Federal Army was spreading all over the country, and I feared to remain where I was. Yet I thought, may I not be in danger in Vicksburg? Suppose the gunboats should make an attack? Still, it was true, as my friend had said, we were in far more danger here from the rabble that usually followed a large army, and who might plunder, insult, and rob us. No; to Vicksburg we must go!

Very hurriedly we made our arrangements, packing with scarcely a moment to lose, not stopping to discuss our sudden move and the alarming news. Our friends, also, were in as great a panic and dismay as ourselves. Mrs. A. had some chests of heavy silver. Many of the pieces were such that it would have taken some time to bury them. Her husband was absent, and she feared to trust the negro men with the secret. Another friend feared to bury her diamonds, thinking in that case she might never see them more; feared, also, to retain them, lest, through negroes' tales, the cupidity of the soldiers might become excited, and she be a sufferer in consequence.

Every tumult in the town caused us to fly to the doors and windows, fearing a surprise at any time; and not only ladies, with pale faces and anxious eyes, met us at every turn, but gentlemen of anti-military dispositions were running hither and thither, with carpet bags and little valises, seeking conveyances, determined to find a safe place, if one could be found, where the sound of a gun or the smell of powder might never disturb them anymore; and, as they ran, each had an alarming report to circulate; so that with the rush and roar of dray, wagon, and carriage, the distracting reports of the rapid advance of the Federal Army, and the stifling clouds of dust that arose—with all, we were in a fair way to believe ourselves any being or object but ourselves.

The depot was crowded with crushing and elbowing human beings, swaying to and fro—baggage being thrown hither and thither—horses wild with fright, and negroes with confusion; and so we found ourselves in a car, amid the living stream that flowed and surged along—seeking the Mobile cars—seeking the Vicksburg cars—seeking anything to bear them away from the threatened and fast depopulating town.

CHAPTER 5

To Vicksburg Again

Leaving the threatened, teeming town behind us, we moved slowly on—our friends, my little one, and myself—toward Vicksburg. Ah! Vicksburg, our city of refuge, the last to yield thou wilt be; and within thy homes we will not fear the footstep of the victorious army, but rest in safety amid thy hills! and those whom we love so dearly will comfort and sustain us in our frightened and panic-stricken condition—will laugh away our woman's fears, and lighten our hearts from the dread and suffering we have experienced. Yet, is there any place where one is perfectly safe in these terrible times? As we travelled along, the night air blowing so refreshingly upon us through the open window—our seats so quiet—the motion of the cars so soothing, my friends soon gave unmistakable signs of the deep sleep that had fallen upon them;—the quiet of the night—the air so fragrant—the heavens above us so calm and starlit!

I leaned my head against the window and looked into the darkness. How calm and earnest the thoughts that came to me after the unquiet and restlessness of the day! The blessed hope of the heavenly home seemed doubly gracious. How longingly I looked upon the veil that lay between our world and the beyond! Ah! the beyond, where Christ has gone, that our life there may be perfected through him; the beyond, where many a night like this my eyes have looked upon the stars; and my soul trembled and panted, wistfully longing for more knowledge of the life above—wistfully longing for the child, the martyr child, that suffered and died upon my bosom— the child whose life on earth was so much a part of my own!—whose heavenly life I wish so much to influence my own!

And I seek, I know not what, as I gaze upon those worlds above. I dare not ask for a revelation; but, ah! could I penetrate beyond the stars and catch one ray of the glorious life! Yet, the consciousness of a refined and purer existence is ever near me, as my mind separates from the earth—gives itself up to intangible and yearning inquiries, that will never be satisfied until I, too, stand within the presence of my Creator. Oh, this night time, this starlit, clear, and most pure heaven before us! Does not one see oneself more clearly, when looking upward with the ever-undefined emotion that we feel when gazing at the heavens at night?—does not our own unworthiness, our soul's need of a Saviour, come to us as our conscience, overcoming the callousness of the day and the world, whispers to us of many derelictions from our duty? of prayers hastily said over? of opportunities for good to our fellow men lost?

The soft answer, the kind word and cheering smile to the world weary, all have been passed by; and we see where good, to one "of the least of these," might have made a life happier; and, as to the pure, all things are pure, so we, as we pant for the heavenly life, and the ennobling existence belonging to it, see more clearly the imperfections in this, and in our daily duties, and our need of a Mediator with him to whose pure eyes we are wholly unworthy; alas! so unworthy, that with this life our worthiness can never begin.

As we passed along nearing Vicksburg, we could see camps and camp fires, with the dim figures of men moving around them; we could see the sentinel guarding the Black River bridge, silent and erect, looking in the darkness like a dusky statue ornamenting some quaint and massive bridge of the old countries; and farther, masses of men in the road marching quietly in the night time, followed by the artillery; long lines of wagons, too, passing through the ravines—now the white covers seen on the brow of the hill; losing sight of them again, we hear the shout of the teamsters, the crack of the whip—and again catch sight of a white top through trees—and the occasional song of a wagoner. At the depot soldiers were crowded, waiting to go out; and on our arrival at our friend's, we, so weary with the excitement and turmoil of the day, were glad to rest our tired heads in calmness and peace, with no fears for the morrow, or restless forebodings of evil.

Upon reading the papers the next morning, almost the first article that caught my eye was an order from General Pemberton, insisting on all non-combatants leaving the city. "Heretofore," he said, "I have merely requested that it should be done; now I demand it."

"Ah!" cried I, "have we no rest for the sole of our foot? Must we again go through the fright and anxiety of yesterday?"

"We cannot leave here," replied my friend. "Where can we go? Here we are among our friends—we are welcome, and we feel in safety. Let us at least share the fate of those we love so much. If we leave, we cannot tell to what we may be exposed—even now, probably, the Federal Army occupy Jackson; if we go into the country, we are liable at any time to be surrounded by them; and to whom can we apply for protection from the soldiery? We *must* stay here, even if the gentlemen say go, which, I fear, they will; we must urge them to allow us to remain, for you know they can refuse us nothing. Oh, we are so quiet and peaceful, we must stay, come what will."

When the gentlemen came, we talked of the "order" with them. At first they said we must leave; but we entreated them to let us stay, representing our deplorable condition in a country overrun by soldiers, the great danger of trying to go to Mobile by railway, the track having been partly destroyed between Meridian and Jackson. We declared that we would almost starve—that we would meet any evil cheerfully in Vicksburg, where our friends were—where we were carefully housed, quiet, and contented. So, laughingly, they said they were completely overcome by our distress, and would arrange it so that we could stay if we wished. "But, remember," they said, "if trouble comes, you must meet it with your eyes open."

"Yes," we said, "we can meet trouble where you are, cheerfully." All seemed to think that the matter would be decided some distance from Vicksburg, and that General Pemberton wanted to cast the responsibility from his shoulders, if the worst came, and ladies were endangered in the city.

CHAPTER 6

Rumours of the Federal Advance on Black River

We settled ourselves delightfully. With our sewing in the morning, and rides in the evening, our home was very pleasant—very happy and quiet. Rumours came to us of the advance of the Federal troops on Black River; yet, so uncertain were the tidings, and so slow was the advantage gained, we began to doubt almost everything. M—— was stationed below at Warrenton, and came only occasionally to see us, as the gunboats were threatening that point. Still, we were in a manner already cut off from the outer world, for the cars had ceased running farther than the Black River bridge, where General Pemberton had stationed his forces, fortifying and awaiting an attack; still, every morning the papers would tell us all was right, and our life passed on the same.

Almost every day we walked up the Sky Parlor Hill, and looked through the glass at the Federal encampment near the head of the abandoned canal; we could see plainly, also, below, at a point called "Brown and Johnson's Landing," the passing of trains of wagons carrying supplies to the fleet below; we could, also, discern troops and mounted men on the opposite shore, though some miles away;—again, at the head of the canal, out in the stream, listlessly lay the dark forms of the gunboats—now two lying quite near each other—then, perhaps, a group of three, or often one alone, manned by negroes, as with the aid of the glass we could see them passing to and fro; we could see, also, the little tugboats carrying despatches from one to the other, we supposed, as frequently after their visit a transport or gunboat would put on steam and follow them up the river; we could see couriers galloping from groups of tents along the shore up to where, we presumed, the masses of the soldiers were encamped.

Altogether, the Federal encampment and movements were far more stirring and interesting than the quiet fortified life of Vicksburg, waiting with calm and bristling front the result of the energetic movements beyond. We met frequently on Sky Parlor Hill an acquaintance on General Pemberton's staff, who seemed to watch with interest operations on the shore above and below us. We could see that Vicksburg was as attentively observed by the Federal troops.

The gunboats that stood out in the stream above seemed to be acting as sentinels, or on a kind of picket duty, I might call it, as a man in uniform constantly paced the deck with a large glass under his arm, which he frequently raised and took a survey of the city. But Vicksburg must have been a sealed book to him among her hills from that point of view.

One night we heard heavy cannonading an hour or two, ceasing, and then commencing again quite early in the morning, undoubtedly from the vicinity of Warrenton. How little we thought that was the commencement of music that would ring in our ears for weeks to come!—how little we thought it the beginning of trouble! That night the sky in the south was crimsoned by the light of a large fire—the cause we could not learn. The next day we heard that the little village of Warrenton had been burned by shells thrown from the boats. M—— came in that evening, and told us that the gunboats had been amusing themselves by throwing shot and shell at the fort—that very little damage had been done, except setting fire to some of the cotton composing the fort, which was still smouldering and burning slowly under the earthworks.

We were told soon after by some of our friends, that the fort at Warrenton had been quietly evacuated; at least, all the guns had been taken from it and brought into Vicksburg, with ammunition, stores, &c.; the troops were left there as a blind for the time being—all this M—— did not tell me. It must have been a trial for the men to lie perfectly quiet, enduring a steady fire that they were unable to return. However, the time came when these men could look back to the shelling of Warrenton as a slight matter in comparison with the storm of shot and shell that rained upon them in the rear of Vicksburg. And now began my excitement: M—— was below, and exposed to the firing we heard every morning and evening; and I prayed for him so fervently, feeling how utterly powerless I was, and how merciful and powerful our Father would be.

Saturday came, and with it the news that a battle was going on between the Federal troops and General Pemberton's forces at Black River; and I saw the blanching of a bright cheek, and felt, with a heavy heart, that the hopes of happiness, for many a year to come, of a dear friend, hung upon a life that would be bravely ventured there today. Oh! the terrible suspense of that day, when feeling that, let the result be what it would (and we trembled for it), the lives of our friends were all in all to us.

CHAPTER 7

The Demoralized Army

Sunday, the 11th.—the memorable seventeenth of May—as we were dressing for church, and had nearly completed the arrangement of shawls and gloves, we heard the loud booming of cannon. Frightened, for at this time we knew not *what* "an hour would bring forth," seeing no one who might account for the sudden alarm, we walked down the street, hoping to find some friend that could tell us if it were dangerous to remain away from home at church. I feared leaving my little one for any length of time, if there were any prospect of an engagement. After walking a square or two, we met an officer, who told us the report we heard proceeded from our own guns, which were firing upon a party of soldiers, who were burning some houses on the peninsula on the Louisiana shore; he told us, also, it had been rumoured that General Pemberton had been repulsed—that many citizens had gone out to attend to the wounded of yesterday's battle—all the ministers and surgeons that could leave had also gone.

Still, as the bell of the Methodist Church rang out clear and loud, my friend and I decided to enter, and were glad that we did so, for we heard words of cheer and comfort in this time of trouble. The speaker was a traveller, who supplied the pulpit this day, as the pastor was absent ministering to the wounded and dying on the battle field. This was a plain man, of simple, fervent words, but with so much of heart in all his exercises, that we felt, after the last hymn had been sung, the last prayer said, that we had been in a purer atmosphere. After the blessing, he requested the ladies to meet and make arrangements for lint and bandages for the wounded.

As we returned home, we passed groups of anxious men at the corners, with troubled faces; very few soldiers were seen; some battery men and officers, needed for the river defences, were passing hastily up the street. Yet, in all the pleasant air and sunshine of the day, an anxious gloom seemed to hang over the faces of men: a sorrowful waiting for tidings, that all knew now, would tell of disaster. There seemed no life in the city; sullen and expectant seemed the men—tearful and hopeful the women—prayerful and hopeful, I might add; for, many a mother, groaning in spirit over the uncertainty of the welfare of those most dear to her, knelt and laid her sorrows at the foot of that Throne, where no earnest suppliant is ever rejected; where the sorrow of many a broken heart has been turned in resignation, to His will who afflicts not willingly the children of men.

And so, in all the dejected uncertainty, the stir of horsemen and wheels began, and wagons came rattling down the street—going rapidly one way, and then returning, seemingly, without aim or purpose: now and then a worn and dusty soldier would be seen passing with his blanket and canteen; soon, straggler after straggler came by, then groups of soldiers worn and dusty with the long march. "What can be the matter?" we all cried, as the streets and pavements became full of these worn and tired-looking men. We sent down to ask, and the reply was: "We are whipped; and the Federals are after us." We hastily seized veils and bonnets, and walked down the avenue to the iron railing that separates the yard from the street.

"Where are you going?" we asked.

No one seemed disposed to answer the question. An embarrassed, pained look came over some of the faces that were raised to us; others seemed only to feel the weariness of the long march; again we asked:

"Where on earth are you going?"

At last one man looked up in a half-surly manner, and answered: "We are running."

"From whom?" exclaimed one of the young girls of the house.

"The Feds, to be sure," said another, half laughing and half shamefaced.

"Oh! shame on you!" cried the ladies; "and you running!"

"It's all Pem's fault," said an awkward, long-limbed, weary-looking man.

"It's all your own fault. Why don't you stand your ground?" was the reply.

"Shame on you all!" cried some of the ladies across the street, becoming excited.

I could not but feel sorry for the poor worn fellows, who did seem indeed heartily ashamed of themselves: some without arms, having

31

probably lost them in the first break of the companies.

"We are disappointed in you!" cried some of the ladies. "Who shall we look to now for protection?"

"Oh!" said one of them, "it's the first time I ever ran. We are Georgians, and we never ran before; but we saw them all breaking and running, and we could not bear up alone."

We asked them if they did not want water; and some of them came in the yard to get it. The lady of the house offered them some supper; and while they were eating, we were so much interested, that we stood around questioning them about the result of the day. "It is all General Pemberton's fault," said a sergeant. "I'm a Missourian, and our boys stood it almost alone, not knowing what was wanted to be done; yet, fighting as long as possible, every one leaving us, and we were obliged to fall back. You know, madam, we Missourians always fight well, even if we have to retreat afterward."

"Oh!" spoke up an old man, "we would ha' fit well; but General Pemberton came up and said: 'Stand your ground, boys. Your General Pemberton is with you;' and then, bless you, lady! the next we see'd of him, he was sitting on his horse behind a house—close, too, at that; and when we see'd that, we thought 'tain't no use, if he's going to sit there."

We could not help, laughing at the old man's tale and his anger. Afterward we were told that General Pemberton behaved with courage—that the fault lay in the arrangement of troops.

And where these weary and worn-out men were going, we could not tell. I think they did not know themselves.

CHAPTER 8

Fresh Troops from Warrenton for the Intrenchments

At dark the fresh troops from Warrenton marched by, going out to the intrenchments in the rear of the city about two miles; many, of the officers were fearful that the fortifications, being so incomplete, would be taken, if the Federal troops pushed immediately on, following their advantage.

As the troops from Warrenton passed by, the ladies waved their handkerchiefs, cheering them, and crying:

"These are the troops that have not run. You'll stand by us, and protect us, won't you? You won't *retreat* and bring the Federals behind you."

And the men, who were fresh and lively, swung their hats, and promised to die for the ladies—never to run—never to retreat; while the poor fellows on the pavement, sitting on their blankets—lying on the ground—leaning against trees, or anything to rest their wearied bodies, looked on silent and dejected. They were not to blame, these poor, weary fellows. If they were unsuccessful, it is what many a man has been before them; and then, endurance of the long fasts in the rifle pits, and coolness amid the showers of ball and shell thrown at devoted Vicksburg afterward, show us that men, though unfortunate, can retrieve their character.

"There has been many a life lost today," said a soldier to me—"many an officer and man."

"Ah! truly, yes," I said; for the ambulances had been passing with wounded and dead; and one came slowly by with officers riding near it, bearing the dead body of General Tilghman, the blood dripping slowly from it. We were told, also, of a friend who had been mortally wounded.

What a sad evening we spent—continually hearing of friends and acquaintances left dead on the field, or mortally wounded, and being brought in ambulances to the hospital! We almost feared to retire that night; no one seemed to know whether the Federal Army was advancing or not; some told us that they were many miles away, and others that they were quite near. How did we know but in the night we might be awakened by the tumult of their arrival!

The streets were becoming quiet; the noise and bustle had died out with the excitement of the day, and, save now and then the rapid passing of some officer, or army wagon, they were almost deserted. And what will the morrow bring forth? I thought, as I leaned from the balcony of my room; will these streets echo to the tread of the victorious army? I shrank from the thought. Without protectors, what might be our fate?—to be turned from our homes, perhaps, widows and orphans. But the heavens above so calm—so smooth and soothing—the quiet glide of the silent river—and the wind swaying the trees with a monotonous wave—quelled and laid these thoughts of evil; and the blessed trust and faith in Him who is all powerful came with renewed balm to my anxious heart.

CHAPTER 9

The Ball in Motion

The next morning all was quiet; we heard no startling rumours; the soldiers were being gathered together and taken out into the rifle pits; Vicksburg was regularly besieged, and we were to stay at our homes and watch the progress of the battle. The rifle pits and intrenchments were almost two miles from the city. We would be out of danger, so we thought; but we did not know what was in preparation for us around the bend of the river. The day wore on; still all was quiet. At night our hopes revived: the Federal troops had not yet come up—another calm night and morning. At three o'clock that evening, the artillery boomed from the intrenchments, roar after roar, followed by the rattle of musketry: the Federal forces were making their first attack. Looking out from the back veranda, we could plainly see the smoke before the report of the guns reached us. Our anxiety was great, indeed, having been told by gentlemen the night before, that the works in the rear of Vicksburg were anything but of a superior kind.

The discharges of musketry were irregular. Yet, to us who were thinking of the dear ones exposed to this frequent firing, the restless forebodings and unhappiness caused by the distant din of battle pained us indeed. After listening for some time to the reports, which sounded to us, in the distance, like the quick, successive droppings of balls on sheet iron, again and again sounded the cannon like thunderings near us. At every report our hearts beat quicker. The excitement was intense in the city. Groups of people stood on every available position where a view could be obtained of the distant hills, where the jets of white smoke constantly passed out from among the trees.

Some of our friends proposed going for a better view up on the balcony around the cupola of the court house. The view from there was most extensive and beautiful. Hill after hill arose in the distance, enclosing the city in the form of a crescent. Immediately in the centre and east of the river, the firing seemed more continuous, while to the left and running northly, the rattle and roar would be sudden, sharp, and vigorous, then ceasing for some time. The hills around near the city, and indeed every place that seemed commanding and secure, was covered with anxious spectators—many of them ladies—fearing the result of the afternoon's conflict. To the extreme left and north, near the river, the warfare became general, while toward the centre the firing became less rapid.

What a beautiful landscape lay out before us! Far in the distance lay the cultivated hills—some already yellow with grain, while on other hills and in the Valleys the deep green of the trees formed the shadows in the fair landscape.

It was amid the clump of trees on the far distant hillside, that the Federal batteries could be discerned by the frequent puffings of smoke from the guns. Turning to the river, we could see a gunboat that had the temerity to come down as near the town as possible, and lay just out of reach of the Confederate batteries, with steam up.

Two more lay about half a mile above and nearer the canal; two or three transports had gotten up steam, and lay near the month of the canal. Below the city a gunboat had come up and landed, out of reach, on the Louisiana side, striving to engage the lower batteries of the town—firing about every fifteen minutes. While we were looking at the river, we saw two large yawls start out from shore, with two larger boats tied to them, and full of men.

We learned that they were the Federal prisoners that had been held in the town, and today paroled and sent over to the Federal encampment, so that the resources of the garrison might be husbanded as much as possible, and the necessity of sustaining them avoided.

The idea made me serious. We might look forward truly now to perhaps real suffering.

Yet, I did not regret my resolution to remain, and would have left the town more reluctantly today than ever before, for we felt that now, indeed, the whole country was unsafe, and that our only hope of safety lay in Vicksburg.

The little boats, with their prisoners, had gained the opposite shore; and we could see the liberated men walking along the river bank; we could see, also, the little steamtug coming down, and stopping at the gunboat near the city; it, also, visited the transports and the gunboats near the canal, and then, leaving, steamed with much swiftness up the river toward the month of the Yazoo.

In looking again with a glass in the rear of the city, we could see the Southern soldiers working at their guns, and walking in the rear of a fort on a hill nearer by. The Federal troops were too distant to discern.

Some ambulances were coming into the city, probably bringing the wounded from the field.

We saw an officer coming in with his head bound up and his arm in a sling, his servant walking by his side leading his horse. Aside from the earnest group of spectators moving from one place to another, the town seemed perfectly quiet.

Looking again toward the river, the gunboat near the lower batteries kept its old position, slowly firing at the lower part of the city; and far over on the other shore, walking rapidly, I observed the figures of the freed prisoners near the canal, and fast becoming indistinct, even with the aid of a glass.

So twilight began falling over the scene—hushing to an occasional report the noise and uproar of the battlefield—falling softly and silently upon the river—separating us more and more from the raging passions surging around us—bringing only the heaven above us, and the small space of life we occupy, distinctly to our eyes.

CHAPTER 10

Cave Shelter

From gentlemen who called on the evening of the attack in the rear of the town, we learned that it was quite likely, judging from the movements on the river, that the gunboats would make an attack that night. We remained dressed during the night; once or twice we sprang to our feet, startled by the report of a cannon; but after waiting in the darkness of the veranda for some time, the perfect quiet of the city convinced us that our alarm was needless.

Next day, two or three shells were thrown from the battlefield, exploding near the house. This was our first shock, and a severe one. We did not dare to go in the back part of the house all day.

Some of the servants came and got down by us for protection, while others kept on with their work as if feeling a perfect contempt for the shells.

In the evening we were terrified and much excited by the loud rush and scream of mortar shells; we ran to the small cave near the house, and were in it during the night, by this time wearied and almost stupefied by the loss of sleep.

The caves were plainly becoming a necessity, as some persons had been killed on the street by fragments of shells. The room that I had so lately slept in had been struck by a fragment of a shell during the first night, and a large hole made in the ceiling. I shall never forget my extreme fear during the night, and my utter hopelessness of ever seeing the morning light. Terror stricken, we remained crouched in the cave, while shell after shell followed each other in quick succession. I endeavoured by constant prayer to prepare myself for the sudden death I was almost certain awaited me. My heart stood still as we would hear the reports from the guns, and the rushing and fearful sound of the shell as it came toward us.

As it neared, the noise became more deafening; the air was full of the rushing sound; pains darted through my temples; my ears were fall of the confusing noise; and, as it exploded, the report flashed through my head like an electric shock, leaving me in a quiet state of terror the most painful that I can imagine—cowering in a corner, holding my child to my heart—the only feeling of my life being the choking throbs of my heart, that rendered me almost breathless. As singly they fell short, or beyond the cave, I was aroused by a feeling of thankfulness that was of short duration. Again and again the terrible fright came over us in that night.

I saw one fall in the road without the mouth of the cave, like a flame of fire, making the earth tremble, and, with a low, singing sound, the fragments sped on in their work of death.

Morning found us more dead than alive, with blanched faces and trembling lips. We were not reassured on hearing, from a man who took refuge in the cave, that a mortar shell in falling would not consider the thickness of earth above us a circumstance.

Some of the ladies, more courageous by daylight, asked him what he was in there for, if that was the case. He was silenced for an hour, when he left. As the day wore on, and we were still preserved, though the shells came as ever, we were somewhat encouraged.

The next morning we heard that Vicksburg would not in all probability hold out more than a week or two, as the garrison was poorly provisioned; and one of General Pemberton's staff officers told us that the effective force of the garrison, upon being estimated, was found to be fifteen thousand men; General Loring having been cut off after the battle of Black River, with probably ten thousand.

The ladies all cried, "Oh, never surrender!" but after the experience of the night, I really could not tell what I wanted, or what my opinions were.

How often I thought of M—— upon the battlefield, and his anxiety for us in the midst of this unanticipated danger, wherein the safety lay entirely on the side of the belligerent gentlemen, who were shelling us so furiously, at least two miles from the city, in the bend of the river near the canal.

So constantly dropped the shells around the city, that the inhabitants all made preparations to live under the ground during the siege. M—— sent over and had a cave made in a hill nearby. We seized the opportunity one evening, when the gunners were probably at their supper, for we had a few moments of quiet, to go over and take posses-

sion. We were under the care of a friend of M——, who was paymaster on the staff of the same general with whom M—— was adjutant. We had neighbours on both sides of us; and it would have been an amusing sight to a spectator to witness the domestic scenes presented without by the number of servants preparing the meals under the high bank containing the caves.

Our dining, breakfasting, and supper hours were quite irregular. When the shells were falling fast, the servants came in for safety, and our meals waited for completion some little time; again they would fall slowly, with the lapse of many minutes between, and out would start the cooks to their work.

Some families had light bread made in large quantities, and subsisted on it with milk (provided their cows were not killed from one milking time to another), without any more cooking, until called on to replenish. Though most of us lived on corn bread and bacon, served three times a day, the only luxury of the meal consisting in its warmth, I had some flour, and frequently had some hard, tough, biscuit made from it, there being no soda or yeast to be procured. At this time we could, also, procure beef. A gentleman friend was kind enough to offer me his camp bed, a narrow spring mattress, which fitted within the contracted cave very comfortably; another had his tent fly stretched over the mouth of our residence to shield us from the sun; and thus I was the recipient of many favours, and under obligations to many gentlemen of the army for delicate and kind attentions; and, in looking back to my trials at that time, I shall ever remember with gratitude the kindness with which they strove to ward off every deprivation.

And so I went regularly to work, keeping house underground. Our new habitation was an excavation made in the earth, and branching six feet from the entrance, forming a cave in the shape of a T. In one of the wings my bed fitted; the other I used as a kind of a dressing room; in this the earth had been cut down a foot or two below the floor of the main cave; I could stand erect here; and when tired of sitting in other portions of my residence, I bowed myself into it, and stood impassively resting at full height—one of the variations in the still shell-expectant life. M——'s servant cooked for us under protection of the hill. Our quarters were close, indeed; yet I was more comfortable than I expected I could have been made under the earth in that fashion.

We were safe at least from fragments of shell—and they were flying in all directions; though no one seemed to think our cave any protection, should a mortar shell happen to fall directly on top of the ground above us. We had our roof arched and braced, the supports of the bracing taking up much room in our confined quarters. The earth was about five feet thick above, and seemed hard and compact; yet, poor M——, every time he came in, examined it, fearing, amid some of the shocks it sustained, that it might crack and fall upon us.

CHAPTER 11

Buried Alive

One afternoon, amid the rush and explosion of the shells, cries and screams arose—the screams of women amid the shrieks of the falling shells. The servant boy, George, after starting and coming back once or twice, his timidity overcoming his curiosity (I was not at all surprised at it), at last gathered courage to go to the ravine near us, from whence the cries proceeded, and found that a negro man had been buried alive within a cave, he being alone at that time. Workmen were instantly set to deliver him, if possible; but when found, the unfortunate man had evidently been dead some little time. His wife and relations were distressed beyond measure, and filled the air with their cries and groans.

This incident made me doubly doubtful of my cave; I feared that I might be buried alive at any time. Another incident happened the same day: A gentleman, resident of Vicksburg, had a large cave made, and repeatedly urged his wife to leave the house and go into it. She steadily refused, and, being quite an invalid, was lying on the bed, when he took her by the hand and insisted upon her accompanying him so strongly, that she yielded; and they had scarcely left the house, when a mortar shell went crashing through, utterly demolishing the bed that had so lately been vacated, tearing up the floor, and almost completely destroying the room.

That night, after my little one had been laid in bed, I sat at the month of the cave, with the servants drawn around me, watching the brilliant display of fireworks the mortar boats were making—the passage of the shell, as it travelled through the heavens, looking like a swiftly moving star. As it fell, it approached the earth so rapidly, that it seemed to leave behind a track of fire.

This night we kept our seats, as they all passed rapidly over us, none falling near. The incendiary shells were still more beautiful in appearance. As they exploded in the air, the burning matter and balls fell like large, clear blue-and-amber stars, scattering hither and thither.

"Miss M——," said one of the more timid servants, "do they want to kill us all dead? Will they keep doing this until we all die?" I said most heartily, "I hope not."

The servants we had with us seemed to possess more courage than is usually attributed to negroes. They seldom hesitated to cross the street for water at any time. The "boy" slept at the entrance of the cave, with a pistol I had given him, telling me I need not be "afeared—dat anyone dat come dar would have to go over his body first."

He never refused to carry out any little article to M—— on the battlefield. I laughed heartily at a dilemma he was placed in one day: The mule that he had mounted to ride out to the battlefield took him to a dangerous locality, where the shells were flying thickly, and then, suddenly stopping, through fright, obstinately refused to stir. It was in vain that George kicked and beat him—go he would not; so, clenching his hand, he hit him severely in the head several times, jumped down, ran home, and left him. The mule stood a few minutes rigidly, then, looking round, and seeing George at some distance from him, turned and followed, quite demurely.

Each day, as the couriers came into the city, M—— would write me little notes, asking after our welfare, and telling me of the progress of the siege. I, in return, would write to him of our safety, but was always careful in speaking of the danger to which we were exposed. I thought poor M—— had enough to try him, without suffering anxiety for us; so I made light of my fears, which were in reality wearing off rapidly. Every week he came in to make inquiries in person. In his letters he charged me particularly to be careful of the provisions—that no one could tell what our necessities might be.

In one of his letters, he says: "Already I am living on pea meal, and cannot think of your coming to this." One thing I had learned quite lately in my cave was to make good bread: one of my cave neighbours had given me yeast and instructions. I, in turn, had instructed a servant, so that when we used the flour it could be presented in a more inviting form.

One morning, after breakfast, the shells began falling so thickly around us, that they seemed aimed at the particular spot on which our cave was located. Two or three fell immediately in the rear of it, exploding a few moments before reaching the ground, and the fragments went singing over the top of our habitation. I, at length, became so much alarmed—as the cave trembled excessively—for our safety, that I determined, rather than be buried alive, to stand out from under the earth; so, taking my child in my arms, and calling the servants, we ran to a refuge near the roots of a large fig tree, that branched out over the bank, and served as a protection from the fragments of shells.

As we stood trembling there—for the shells were falling all around us—some of my gentlemen friends came up to reassure me, telling me that the tree would protect us, and that the range would probably be changed in a short time. While they spoke, a shell, that seemed to be of enormous size, fell, screaming and hissing, immediately before the mouth of our cave, within a few feet of the entrance, sending up a huge column of smoke and earth, and jarring the ground most sensibly where we stood. What seemed very strange, the earth closed in around the shell, and left only the newly upturned soil to show where it had fallen.

Long it was before the range was changed, and the frightful missiles fell beyond us—long before I could resolve to return to our sadly threatened home.

I found on my return that the walls were seamed here and there with cracks, but the earth had remained firm above us. I took possession again, with resignation, yet in fear and trembling.

CHAPTER 12

Fire at Night

My past resolution having forsaken me, again were the mortar shells heard with extreme terror, and I was many days recovering the equanimity I had been so long attaining. This night, as a few nights before, a large fire raged in the town. I was told that a large storehouse, filled with commissary stores, was burning, casting lurid lights over the devoted city; and amid all, fell—with screams and violent explosions, flinging the fatal fragments in all directions—our old and relentless enemies, the mortar shells.

The night was so warm, and the cave so close, that I tried to sit out at the entrance, George saying he would keep watch and tell when they were falling toward us. Soon the report of the gun would be heard, and George, standing on the hillock of loose earth, near the cave, looked intently upward; while I, with suspended breath, would listen anxiously as he cried, "Here she comes! going over!" then again, "Coming—falling—falling right dis way!" Then I would spring to my feet, and for a moment hesitate about the protection of the cave. Suddenly, as the rushing descent was heard, I would beat a precipitate retreat into it, followed by the servants.

That night I could scarcely sleep, the explosions were so loud and frequent. Before we retired, George had been lying without the door. I had arisen about twelve o'clock, and stood looking out at the different courses of light marking the passage of the shells, when I noticed that George was not in his usual place at the entrance. On looking out, I saw that he was sleeping soundly, some little distance off, and many fragments of shell falling near him. I aroused him, telling him to come to the entrance for safety. He had scarcely started, when a huge piece of shell came whizzing along, which fortunately George dodged in time, and it fell in the very spot where he had so lately slept.

Fearing to retire, I sat in the moonlight at the entrance, the square of light that lay in the doorway causing our little bed, with the sleeping child, to be set out in relief against the dark wall of the cave—causing the little mirror and a picture or two I had hung against the wall to show misshapen lengths of shadows—tinting the crimson shawl that draped the entrance of my little dressing room, with light on the outer folds, and darkening in shadow the inner curves;—beautifying all, this silvery glow of moonlight, within the darkened earth—beautifying my heart with lighter and more hopeful thoughts. Whatever the sins of the world may have brought us to—however dark and fearful the life to which man may subject us, our Heavenly Father ever blesseth us alike with the sun's warmth and the moon's beauty—ever blesseth us with the hope that, when our toil and travail here are ended, the peace and the beautiful life of heaven will be ours.

Days wore on, and the mortar shells had passed over continually without falling near us; so that I became quite at my ease, in view of our danger, when one of the Federal batteries opposite the intrenchments altered their range; so that, at about six o'clock every evening, Parrott shells came whirring into the city, frightening the inhabitants of caves woefully.

Our policy in building had been to face directly away from the river, and all caves were prepared, as near as possible, in this manner. As the fragments of shells continued with the same impetus after the explosion, in but one direction, onward, they were not likely to reach us, fronting in this manner with their course.

But this was unexpected—guns throwing shells from the battle field directly at the entrance of our caves. Really, was there to be no mental rest for the women of Vicksburg?

The cave we inhabited was about five squares from the levee. A great many had been made in a hill immediately beyond us; and near this hill we could see most of the shells fall. Caves were the fashion—the rage— over besieged Vicksburg. Negroes, who understood their business, hired themselves out to dig them, at from thirty to fifty dollars, according to the size. Many persons, considering different localities unsafe, would sell them to others, who had been less fortunate, or less provident; and so great was the demand for cave workmen, that a new branch of industry sprang up and became popular—particularly as the personal safety of the workmen was secured, and money withal.

CHAPTER 13

Shells From the Rear of the City

It was about four o'clock, one Wednesday evening—the shelling during the day had gone on about as usual—I was reading in safety, I imagined, when the unmistakable whirring of Parrott shells told us that the battery we so much feared had opened from the intrenchments. I ran to the entrance to call the servants in; and immediately after they entered, a shell struck the earth a few feet from the entrance, burying itself without exploding. I ran to the little dressing room, and could hear them striking around us on all sides. I crouched closely against the wall, for I did not know at what moment one might strike within the cave. A man came in much frightened, and asked to remain until the danger was over. The servants stood in the little niche by the bed, and the man took refuge in the small ell where I was stationed. He had been there but a short time, standing in front of me, and near the wall, when a Parrott shell came whirling in at the entrance, and fell in the centre of the cave before us all, lying there smoking.

Our eyes were fastened upon it, while we expected every moment the terrific explosion would ensue. I pressed my child closer to my heart, and drew nearer to the wall. Our fate seemed almost certain. The poor man who had sought refuge within was most exposed of all. With a sudden impulse, I seized a large double blanket that lay near, and gave it to him for the purpose of shielding him from the fragments; and thus we remained for a moment, with our eyes fixed in terror on the missile of death, when George, the servant boy, rushed forward, seized the shell, and threw it into the street, running swiftly in the opposite direction.

Fortunately, the fuse had become nearly extinguished, and the shell fell harmless—remaining near the mouth of the cave, as a trophy of the fearlessness of the servant and our remarkable escape. Very thankful was I for our preservation, which was the theme of conversation for a day among our cave neighbours. The incident of the blanket was also related; and all laughed heartily at my wise supposition that the blanket could be any protection from the heavy fragments of shells.

E'er was this all: I had occasion to go to the month of the cave one evening to speak to George; and there, with an enlightened audience of servants from the surrounding caves collected near him, George was going through a grave pantomime of the whole affair. It seems that he expected the refugee to act the part of preserver in our extremity, and throw out the shell; but, as he was disappointed in the matter, he represented him in the most ridiculous manner possible to the audience.

Pressing up closely to the wheel of a wagon nearby, George extended his eyes, holding out his hand as if with a shield, and shrinking with the semblance of extreme terror, that amused his spectators vastly: then, changing the whole character, he put on the bravest port imaginable, pushing his hat, with an independent air, on the side of his head; and, assuming a don't-carish look, he sauntered forward to a large piece of shell that lay conveniently near, caught it with both hands, gave it a careless swing and throw far different from the reality, turned on his heels, walked back to the wagon, with the peculiar swinging step of a proud negro; then, leaning his arm on the wheel, carelessly surveyed his audience, with a look that plainly said, "What you think o' dat, niggars?" The benefited group immediately began laughing and applauding, like a well-trained bevy of *claqueurs*, in which they were soon joined by George himself.

Soon after, I received a note from M——, imploring me to be careful and remain within the cave constantly. I could see that he was restless and troubled in regard to the new peril from the battle field.

And so the weary days went on—the long, weary days—when we could not tell in what terrible form death might come to us before the sun went down. Another fear that troubled M—— was, that our provisions might not last us during the siege. He would frequently urge me to husband all that I had, for troublesome times were probably in store for us; told me of the soldiers in the intrenchments, who would have gladly eaten the bread that was left from our meals, for they were suffering every privation, and that our servants lived far better than these men who were defending the city. Soon the pea meal became an article of food for us also, and a very unpalatable article it proved. To make it of proper consistency, we were obliged to mix some corn meal with it, which cooked so much faster than the pea meal, that it burned before the bread was half done. The taste was peculiar and disagreeable.

However, it soon proved unwholesome, for the soldiers were again allowed to draw rations of the remaining corn meal, with the peas in the kernel to be boiled with meat. We were, indeed, experiencing the rigors and hardships of a siege, for we ate nothing now but meat and bread.

Still, we had nothing to complain of in comparison with the soldiers: many of them were sick and wounded in a hospital in the most exposed parts of the city, with shells falling and exploding all around them. One shell went completely through a hospital in the centre of the city, without exploding or injuring any one, save by the severe shock to the invalids: a fragment afterward came through the side of the same house, severely fracturing the hip of a soldier, who was lying already wounded; one or two wounded men were, also, killed by fragments of shell while in the hospital.

CHAPTER 14

Descent of a Shell Through a Cave

Even the very animals seemed to share the general fear of a sadden and frightful death. The dogs would be seen in the midst of the noise to gallop up the street, and then to return, as if fear had maddened them. On hearing the descent of a shell, they would dart aside—then, as it exploded, sit down and howl in the most pitiful manner. There were many walking the street, apparently without homes. George carried on a continual warfare with them, as they came about the fire where our meals were cooking.

In the midst of other miserable thoughts, it came into my mind one day, that these dogs through hunger might become as much to be dreaded as wolves. Groundless was this anxiety, for in the course of a week or two they had almost disappeared.

The horses, belonging to the officers, and fastened to the trees near the tents, would frequently strain the halter to its fall length, rearing high in the air, with a loud snort of terror, as a shell would explode near. I could hear them in the night cry out in the midst of the uproar, ending in a low, plaintive whinny of fear.

The poor creatures subsisted entirely on cane tops and mulberry leaves. Many of the mules and horses had been driven outside of the lines, by order of General Pemberton, for subsistence. Only mules enough were left, belonging to the Confederacy, to allow three full teams to a regiment. Private property was not interfered with.

Sitting in the cave, one evening, I heard the most heartrending screams and moans. I was told that a mother had taken a child into a cave about a hundred yards from us; and having laid it on its little bed, as the poor woman believed, in safety, she took her seat near the entrance of the cave. A mortar shell came rushing through the air, and fell with much force, entering the earth above the sleeping child—cutting through into the cave—oh! most horrible sight to the mother—crushing in the upper part of the little sleeping head, and taking away the young innocent life without a look or word of passing love to be treasured in the mother's heart.

I sat near the square of moonlight, silent and sorrowful, hearing the sobs and cries—hearing the moans of a mother for her dead child—the child that a few moments since lived to caress and love—speaking the tender words that endear so much the tie of mother and child. Oh, the little lonely grave! so far distant, yet so ever present with me; the sunny, auburn head that I laid there six months after this terrible war began!

I could not hear those sobs and cries without thinking of the night—that last night—when I held my darling to my heart, thinking that, though so suddenly stricken and so scared, she would still live to bless my life. And the terrible awakening!—to find that, lying in my arms all my own, as I believed, she was going swiftly—going into the far unknown eternity! Sliding from my embrace, the precious life was called by One so mighty—so all-powerful—yet so merciful, that I bowed my head in silence.

Still the moans from the bereaved mother came borne on the pleasant air, floating through the silvery moonlit scene—saddening hearts that had never known sorrow, and awakening chords of sympathy in hearts that before had thrilled and suffered. Yet, "it is better to have loved and lost than never to have loved at all." Yes, better the tender memory of a hidden life that glows in onr hearts forever; better, all will say who have known the light and consolation given from on high, when we throw ourselves before His Throne in utter wretchedness, and arise strong—strong in the strength that never faileth—the Lord's strength. The desert that hath not known the oases of life, though blasted and withered by the burning *sirocco* that passeth over, cannot know the refreshing and gentle drops that bring renewed and more tender verdure.

How very sad this life in Vicksburg!—how little security can we feel, with so many around us seeing the morning light that will never more see the night! I could not sit quietly within hearing of so much grief; and, leaving my seat, I paced backward and forward before the low entrance of my house. The court-house bell tolled twelve; and though the shells fell slowly still around the spot where the young life had gone out, yet friends were going to and from the place.

How blightingly the hand of warfare lay upon the town! even in the softening light of the moon—the closed and desolate houses—the gardens, with gates half open, and cattle standing amid the loveliest flowers and verdure! This carelessness of appearance and evident haste of departure was visible everywhere—the inhabitants, in this perilous time, feeling only anxiety for personal safety and the strength of their cave homes.

The moans of pain came slowly and more indistinct, until all was silent; and the bereaved mother slept, I hope—slept to find, on waking, a dull pressure of pain at her heart, and in the first collection of faculties will wonder what it is. Then her care for the child will return, and the new sorrow will again come to her—gone, forever gone!

It will take days to fully realize it, and then she will struggle and grow strong. God in his mercy helps the poor human hearts that suffer, struggle, and grow strong in these sad years of warfare! No one came now—no word to show that life still throbbed in the silent city.

The fresh air told of the coming morning: the guns were still. Peace for a short time reigned in the troubled city; and, in the perfect quiet that prevailed, my eyes grew heavy, and I once more sought my bed—this time to rest peacefully until the cheerful morning light dawned upon us.

Chapter 15

Sinking of the "Cincinnati"

With the dawn came the old unrest and distrust, for the shells were again falling quite thickly around us; and I passed an hour or two in continual shrinkings and exclamations. At length our tormentors passed farther on, and I again felt relieved from anxiety.

At ten or twelve o'clock, we saw, in spite of the continual falling of the shells, gentlemen hurrying toward the river. Soon we heard the Confederate river batteries booming loudly, and then all was silent. What could it mean? I did not venture to look without; and so I sat waiting for someone to come to me. At last a friend appeared, who, in the most triumphant manner, told us that the Confederates had routed the Federal fleet. The gunboats had formed in line of battle, sailing down majestically, with the *Cincinnati*—one of the finest boats in the river navy—leading the attack.

She came rapidly down around the point of the peninsula—the signal guns silent—when the battery, containing the Brooks gun, opened on her, as she came within range. The first shot cut down the flag; the second struck her side; and the third, the Brooks ball, with the steel wedge, cut into the iron plates near the water's edge. She turned immediately, and steamed back up the river in a sinking condition. The remaining boats, also, changed their course and retired. The *Cincinnati* had scarcely turned the point, when she sank near the shore.

"Ah! Yes!" said the major, "had it not been for the fortunate sinking of the *Cincinnati*, you would have become conscious of a fearful warfare raging in the city. Had the boats gotten opposite and engaged our batteries, the firing would have been terrific."

The major also told us that many ladies had been so much interested in the expected engagement, that they had gone up on Sky Parlor Hill for a better view.

54

It has been said that the Federal guns have never been sufficiently elevated to throw shell and shot so high as Sky Parlor Hill; yet, I should not like to risk my life for mere curiosity sake, when it was not possible to be of any service.

The Sky Parlor Hill is so called from its extreme height, being a portion of the bluff that stood where the principal commercial street now stands, the grading of the city having taken most of the elevation down. The hill now occupies about a square—the distance of two squares from the river—and is a prominent feature from all parts of the city. A rugged drive winds on one side up the steep ascent, and a long and dizzy flight of wooden steps ascend from the street on the opposite side.

It is surmounted by a little house that one could imagine surmounted "the bean stalk," in the celebrated history of "Jack," quaint and old, yet one that the earlier inhabitants would have called a "fine house."

The view—and that is what the place is visited for—is good, both of the city and river, for some miles above. Crowds of people collect here on the occasion of any move being made in the direction of the river.

A large trunk was picked up after the sinking of the *Cincinnati*, belonging to a surgeon on board. It contained valuable surgical instruments that could not be procured in the Confederacy; a letter, also, written to the gentleman's wife previous to the departure of the fleet from above, telling her that the letter would be mailed at Vicksburg, as there was no doubt whatever that the place would be taken when an attack was made from the river.

It was also said that Commodore Porter was aboard the *Cincinnati*. How the fact was ascertained, no one could tell.

Shortly after the sinking of the *Cincinnati*, I received a note from M——, saying that he was very much troubled in regard to our safety in the city—fearing that some time a mortar shell might fall on our cave, or that the constant jarring of the earth from the near explosion might cause it to seam and fall upon us. Therefore, he had decided to have a home made for me near the battlefield, where he was stationed—one that would be entirely out of reach of the mortar shells. I was positively shocked at the idea—going to the battlefield! where ball and shell fell without intermission. Was M—— in earnest? I could scarcely believe it.

A friend came soon after, and told me that I would find my home on the battlefield far more pleasant and safe than the one in town—that we were protected from the fragments only in our cave—that on the battlefield the missiles were of far less weight, and in falling far less dangerous.

We were to experience our last and nearest explosion of the never-to-be-forgotten mortar shells before we left. M—— had written to me to be ready on the following night. As the moon was not shining, the firing from the Federal batteries would cease at dark; afterward we could go out without interruption. I was delighted at the prospect of a change in our mouldy lives, and looked forward to our ride—after dark though it was—with the utmost pleasure.

CHAPTER 16

Fall of a Shell at the Corner of My Cave

I was sitting near the entrance, about five o'clock, thinking of the pleasant change—oh, bless me!—that tomorrow would bring, when the bombardment commenced more furiously than usual, the shells falling thickly around us, causing vast columns of earth to fly upward, mingled with smoke. As usual, I was uncertain whether to remain within or run out. As the rocking and trembling of the earth was very distinctly felt, and the explosions alarmingly near, I stood within the mouth of the cave ready to make my escape, should one chance to fall above our domicile. In my anxiety I was startled by the shouts of the servants and a most fearful jar and rocking of the earth, followed by a deafening explosion, such as I had never heard before. The cave filled instantly with powder smoke and dust.

I stood with a tingling, prickling sensation in my head, hands, and feet, and with a confused train. Yet alive!—was the first glad thought that came to me;—child, servants, all here, and saved!—from some great danger, I felt. I stepped out, to find a group of persons before my cave, looking anxiously for me; and lying all around, freshly torn, rose bushes, *arbor-vitæ* trees, large clods of earth, splinters, pieces of plank, wood, &c. A mortar shell had struck the corner of the cave, fortunately so near the brow of the hill, that it had gone obliquely into the earth, exploding as it went, breaking large masses from the side of the hill—tearing away the fence, the shrubbery and flowers—sweeping all, like an avalanche, down near the entrance of my good refuge.

I stood dismayed, and surveyed the havoc that had been made around me, while our little family under it all had been mercifully preserved. Though many of the neighbouring servants had been standing near at the time, not one had been injured in the slightest degree; yet, pieces of plank, fragments of earth, and splinters had fallen in all directions. A portion of earth from the roof of my cave had been dislodged and fallen. Saving this, it remained intact.

That evening some friends sat with me: one took up my guitar and played some pretty little airs for as; yet, the noise of the shells threw a discord among the harmonies. To me it seemed like the crushing and bitter spirit of hate near the light and grace of happiness. How could we sing and laugh amid our suffering fellow beings—amid the shriek of death itself?

This, only breaking the daily monotony of our lives!—this thrilling knowledge of sudden and horrible death occurring near us, told tonight and forgotten in tomorrow's renewal!—this sad news of a Vicksburg day! A little negro child, playing in the yard, had found a shell; in rolling and turning it, had innocently pounded the fuse; the terrible explosion followed, showing, as the white cloud of smoke floated away, the mangled remains of a life that to the mother's heart had possessed all of beauty and joy.

A young girl, becoming weary in the confinement of the cave, hastily ran to the house in the interval that elapsed between the slowly falling shells. On returning, an explosion sounded near her—one wild scream, and she ran into her mother's presence, sinking like a wounded dove, the life blood flowing over the light summer dress in crimson ripples from a death-wound in her side, caused by the shell fragment.

A fragment had also struck and broken the arm of a little boy playing near the mouth of his mother's cave. This was one day's account.

I told of my little girl's great distress when the shells fell thickly near us—how she ran to me breathless, hiding her head in my dress without a word; then cautiously looking out, with her anxious face questioning, would say: "Oh! mamma, was it a mortar tell?" Poor children, that their little hearts should suffer and quail amid these daily horrors of war!

The next evening, about four o'clock, M——'s dear face appeared. He told us that he had heard of all the danger through which we had passed, and was extremely anxious to have us out of reach of the mortar shells, and near him; he also thought we would find our new home on the battle field far superior to this; he wished us to go out as soon as possible. As at this hour in the evening, for the last week, the Federal guns had been quiet until almost sundown, he urged me to be ready in the shortest time possible; so I hastened our arrangements, and we soon were in the ambulance, driving with great speed toward the rifle pits.

O the beautiful sunlight and the fresh evening air! How glowing and delightful it all seemed after my incarceration under the earth! I turned to look again and again at the setting sun and the brilliant crimson glow that suffused the atmosphere. All seemed glad and radiant: the sky—the flowers and trees along our drive—the cool and fragrant breeze—all, save now and then the sullen boom of the mortar, as it slowly cast its death-dealing shell over the life we were leaving behind us.

"Were it not for the poor souls still within, I could have clapped my hands in a glad, defiant jubilee as I heard the reports, for I thought I was leaving my greatest fear of our old enemy in the desolate cave of which I had taken my last contemptuous glance; yet, the fear returned forcibly to me afterward.

CHAPTER 17

Ride to the Fortifications

The road we were travelling was graded out through the hills; and on every side we could see, thickly strewn among the earthy cliffs, the never-to-be-lost sight of caves—large caves and little caves—some cut out substantially, roomy, and comfortable, with braces and props throughout—many only large enough for one man to take refuge in, standing ;— again, at a low place in the earth was a seat for a passer-by in case of danger.

Driving on rapidly, we reached the suburbs of the city, where the road became shady and pleasant—still with caves at every large road excavation, reminding one very much of the numberless holes that swallows make in summer; for both the mortar and Parrott shells disputed this district; and a cave, front in whatever direction it might, was not secure from fragments. M—— impatiently urged on the driver, fearing that when the firing recommenced we would still be on the road.

Suddenly, a turn of the drive brought in sight two large forts on the hills above us; and passing down a ravine near one of these, the ambulance stopped. Here we saw two or three of the little shell and bomb proof-houses in the earth, covered with logs and turf. We were hastily taken out and started for our home, when I heard a cutting of the air—the most expressive term I can use for that peculiar sound—above my head; and the balls dropped thickly around me, bringing leaves and small twigs from the trees with them.

I felt a sudden rush to my heart; but the soldiers were camped near, and many stood cautiously watching the effect of the sudden fall of metal around me. I would not for the world have shown fear; so, braced by my pride, I walked with a firm and steady pace, notwithstanding the treacherous suggestions of my heart that beat a loud

"Run, run." M——, fearing every moment that I might fall by his side, hurried me anxiously along. Within a short distance was the adjutant's office, where we took refuge until the firing became less heavy. Here we found friends, and sat chatting some time.

The "office" was a square excavation made in the side of the hill, covered over with logs and earth, seemingly quite cool and comfortable. I had been confined for so long a time in a narrow space of earth, that daylight, green trees, and ample room became a new pleasure to me. At sundown there was a cessation in the rapid fall of balls and shells; and we again started for our home. I was taken up a little footpath that led from the ravine up under a careless, graceful arch of wild grape vines, whose swinging branchlets were drawn aside; and a low, long room, cut into the hillside and shaded by the growth of forest trees around, was presented to my view as our future home. What a pleasant place, after the close little cave in the city!—large enough for two rooms—the back and sides solid walls of earth, the sloping of the hill bringing down the wall to about four feet at the entrance, leaving the spaces above, between the wall and roof, for light; the side, looking out on the road through the ravine, was entirely open, yet shaded from view by the clustering vines over the pathway.

I took possession delightedly. A blanket, hung across the centre, made us two good-sized rooms: the front room, with a piece of carpet laid down to protect us from the dampness of the floor, and two or three chairs, formed our little parlour; and the back room, quiet and retired, the bedroom. Over the top of the earth, or our house, held up by huge forked props, were the trunks of small trees laid closely across together; over that, brush, limbs, and leaves, and covering all this the thickness of two or three feet of earth beaten down compactly, and thought perfectly safe from Minié balls and Parrott or shrapnel shells.

We had our tent fly drawn over the front, making a very pleasant veranda; for a narrow terrace had been made along the entrance, from which the hill sloped abruptly down to the road in the ravine opposite the dwelling; in the rear the hill rose steeply above us. All was quiet tonight, as it usually is, I was told, when the moon is not brightly shining.

The Federal commanders fear that the Confederates will strive to improve their defences by the moonlight, which is certainly done, firing or not, for the fortifications need constant strengthening, being frequently badly torn by the Parrott shells.

The next morning at four o'clock, I was awakened by a perfect tumult in the air: the explosion of shrapnel and the rattling of shrapnel balls around us reminded me that my dangers and cares were not yet over. How rapidly and thickly the shells and Minié balls fell—Parrott of various sizes—canister and solid shot, until I was almost deafened by the noise and explosions! I lay and thought of the poor soldiers down below in the ravine, with only their tents over their heads; and it seemed in this storm of missiles that all must be killed. How strange so few casualties occur during these projectile storms!

Our little home stood the test nobly. We were in the first line of hills back of the heights that were fortified; and, of course, we felt the full force of the very energetic firing that was constantly kept up; and being so near, many that passed over the first line of hills would fall directly around us.

CHAPTER 18

Horrors of War

How dewy and pleasant the morning! I stood looking out from the little terrace, breathing the fresh air, and learning the new surroundings, so far as my eye went, for it was not safe to venture out from the covering of the cave—the ravine fronting me, shady, dark, and cool—the sun just rising over the hilltop and lighting the upper limbs of the large trees. Up the ravine, the Headquarters, horses were tethered, lazily rising and shaking their coats after the night's rest on the ground—shaking off their drowsiness to begin the breakfast of mulberry leaves. Amidst the constant falling of rifle balls, the birds sang as sweetly, and flew as gayly from tree to tree, as if there were peace and plenty in the land. Plenty there certainly was not in Vicksburg, as anyone would have said who had been invited to our little breakfast that morning: bacon side and bread were all; and I had become so accustomed to them, that I obeyed the calls to breakfast with reluctance; eating, most practically, to sustain life, without the slightest relish for the food I was compelled to masticate and swallow.

Yet, all received their trials with cheerfulness. The gentlemen, who breakfasted with us that morning, laughed and made merry over the rations, and told me of the mule meat that was soon to be served up to us.

They were speaking of a charge that had been made, most gallantly, by General Burbridge and the Federal troops of his command, on the Confederate intrenchments: they had rushed over the breastworks and into the rifle pits, driving out the Southern soldiers. The whole Confederate camp near the spot arose in a furious excitement, officers and men alike throwing hand grenades down upon the intruders, until they were forced to retire, after holding the place some little time. I was told that General Burbridge had, laughingly, remarked to a Confederate officer, during the truce, that, staying in the intrenchments in the hot sun, and having hand grenades thrown at him in profusion, was as warm a work as he wished to undertake in one day.

After the Federal troops left the intrenchments, a hole was found in the loose earth of the breastworks that caused much amusement among the Confederate soldiers—a large hole where one of the Federals had literally burrowed his way out from the pits. "I reckon he's some kin to a mole," sagely commented one of the soldiers.

A flag of truce had been sent by the Federal commander, asking leave to bury the killed and remove the wounded that had been left on the field, in one of the charges that had been made on the Confederate lines.

The request had been refused by General Pemberton. Afterward the effluvia from the dead bodies became so intolerable, that he was obliged in his turn to ask a truce, and request the Federal officers to bury their dead. I was distressed to hear of a young Federal lieutenant who had been severely wounded and left on the field by his comrades. He had lived in this condition from Saturday until Monday, lying in the burning sun without water or food; and the men on both sides could witness the agony of the life thus prolonged, without the power to assist him in any way. I was glad, indeed, when I heard the poor man had expired on Monday morning.

Another soldier left on the field, badly wounded in the leg, had begged most piteously for water; and lying near the Confederate intrenchments, his cries were all directed to the Confederate soldiers. The firing was heaviest where he lay; and it would have been at the risk of a life to have gone to him; yet, a Confederate soldier asked and obtained leave to carry water to him, and stood and fanned him in the midst of the firing, while he eagerly drank from the heroic soldier's canteen.

The officer who related this little incident had not yet obtained the name of the noble man. Truly, "the bravest are the tenderest; the loving are the daring." How generous— how truly brave the man who would thus dare death! who would, at the risk of life, perform a truly Christian deed! Oh! were all men but true followers of the Prince of Peace, how short would be this warfare! Did only individual Christians strive to do their duty in every respect, this great suffering would not be upon us.

There are enough in the world who worship Him who died that all might be happy—enough to stand before the heads of the Christian nation and plead in His name that there be mercy for these dying and bleeding thousands—that these brothers, sons, and husbands may not lie torn, swollen, and writhing in the hot sun, with burning eyes and parched tongues, far, far from those who are powerless to succour them in this fearful time; and, with these pleadings, would ascend prayers to Him who rewards the peacemakers as the children of God—prayers from many an aching, tear-seared heart; and the fierce bitterness, strife, and hatred that move men so, would pale before this blessing. Should they fail, and the wrong go on, then they have done their duty; and they will find mercy, not where the error of man's judgment withholds it, but before Him to whom the least of these are of incalculable value.

One morning George made an important discovery—a newly made stump of *sassafras*, very near the cave, with large roots extending in every direction, affording us an inexhaustible vein of tea for future use. We had been drinking water with our meals previous to this disclosure; coffee and tea had long since been among the things that were, in the army. We, however, were more fortunate than many of the officers, having access to an excellent cistern near us; while many of our friends used muddy water, or river water, which, being conveyed so great a distance, became extremely warm and disagreeable.

CHAPTER 19

An Acceptable Present

A servant brought me one day a present from an officer, that was acceptable indeed: two large, yellow, ripe, June apples, sealed in a large envelope. They were as much of a variety to me as pineapples would have been.

On another occasion, a gentleman sent me four large slices of ham, having been fortunate enough to procure a small piece himself. Now and then gentlemen in calling would bring to my little girl and myself some little article that it was impossible to procure; and only those who have undergone like privations can understand how truly grateful we felt for these little kindnesses. One day a friend brought us some fruit that had been presented to him. While we were conversing, my little hunger-besieged two-year-old daughter quietly secured it, and, sitting on the floor, ate with avidity.

When she had finished nearly all of it, she turned around, with a bright and well-satisfied face, to me, saying, "Mamma, it's so dood"— the first intimation that I had that my portion had disappeared. Dear child; I trembled for her in the greater trials I believed in store for us. Fruits and vegetables were not to be procured at any price. Everyone felt the foreboding of a more serious trouble, the great fear of starvation that stared all in the face causing those who possessed any article in the shape of edibles to retain it for that period to which all looked for- ward with anxiety—when we would come to actual want.

Already the men in the rifle pits were on half rations—flour or meal enough to furnish bread equivalent in quantity to two biscuits in two days: many of them ate it all at once, and the next day fasted, preferring, as they said, to have one good meal.

So they sat cramped up all day in the pits—their rations cooked in the valley and brought to them—scarcely daring to change their positions and stand erect, for the Federal sharpshooters were watching for the heads; and to rise above the breastworks was almost certain death. Frequently, a Parrott shell would penetrate the intrenchments, and, exploding, cause frightful wounds, and death most frequently. "Ah!" said M——, one day, "it is to the noble men in the rifle pits that Vicksburg will owe aught of honour she may gain in this siege. I revere them, as I see them undergoing every privation with courage and patience, anxious only for the high reputation of the city."

They amused themselves, while lying in the pits, by cutting out little trinkets from the wood of the parapet and the Minié balls that fell around them. Major Fry, from Texas, excelled in skill and ready invention, I think: he sent me one day an arm chair that he had cut from a Minié ball—the most minute affair of the kind I ever saw, yet perfectly symmetrical. At another time, he sent me a diminutive plough made from the parapet wood, with traces of lead, and a lead point made from a Minié ball.

I had often remarked how cheerfully the soldiers bore the hardships of the siege. I saw them often passing with their little sacks containing scanty rations, whistling and chatting pleasantly, as around them thickly flew the balls and shells.

Poor men, yet so badly used, and undergoing so many privations!

CHAPTER 20

Dismal Experience

The clouds had been darkening around us all day, and at night we had the prospect of a storm.

M—— sent George out with a spade to slope the earth about the roof of our home, and widen the water ditch around it; yet, it was not until the next morning that the rain began falling. By daylight I heard M—— giving orders rapidly about packing the earth firmly, deepening the ditch, and watching the rear of the cave.

I opened my eyes to see without the darkness and gloom of a rainy day—to feel the dampness of the mist upon my face, and to behold M—— standing at the entrance, with the movable articles near him piled out of reach of the driving rain, giving orders to George in regard to our doubly besieged fortress. I lay and listened to the dropping and plashing with a dreamy pleasure at first; but hearing M—— start out to see if all were right, I sprang up, thinking I might assist in keeping out the water. It was a very fortunate move; for I had scarcely begun dressing, when the earth gave away at the head of my bed, and a perfect spout of muddy water burst through the embankment and fell in the centre of the resting place I had so lately left.

To run and call M—— to stop the water in the back part of the cave, and, in the greatest haste, to assist Cinth in removing every article that was at all dry, and let the water have free course through, was the work of an instant; yet, in the short time that the water had flowed through the cave, we presented a miserably deluged appearance: trunks were piled on trunks—lines hanging from log to log in the roof, filled with the dripping carpet, blankets, sheets, and miscellaneous articles, dripping with a dreary patter on the floor—chairs turned up together, and packed out of the way—our home—like arrangements all in disorder. And now that the water had been turned that flowed through the cave, I and the servant sat, disconsolately, with our skirts drawn around, and our feet on little blocks of wood to keep them out of the mad, with rueful faces, regarding the sweeping of the water and plashing of rain without.

The water, having overflowed the sides of the ditch, making a new channel, and pouring down at the entrance, had completely washed away our little terrace, leaving a huge and yawning gulf immediately in front of us. I was thus contemplating, sorrowfully, the ruins of our little home, when M—— came down, bringing cheer to us again in the expression of his bright, strong, and calm face; the water was flowing in little streams from his hat down to his coat, flowing over his coat, making little pools on the floor as he stood. He declared that the storm was nearly over, and that we would have some breakfast in spite of it.

Taking his hat from his head and shaking the water from it, and from his hair, he bade George take his spade and cut a fireplace near the entrance, bring up his camp kettles, which were full of water, kindle a large fire, and have the breakfast on. He congratulated me upon the perfect safety of our residence, that the water was running around it in regular Venetian style, and that for the present we were perfectly waterproof.

Indeed, our home was in a precarious situation on a rainy day, for we were planted in the bed of the torrent of water that drained. from the hill above; yet, M—— assured me that now we had nothing to fear, for with George he had packed the earth perfectly firm and secure. He laughed heartily at my narrow escape; for I declared that I should never have felt in a pleasant humour again if that rush of muddy water had fallen on me.

Soon the fire blazed cheerfully up, and George commenced the preparation of our simple breakfast—M—— going out to attend to some reports. I had always looked forward to the prospect of rain with pleasure, as procuring us some respite from the incessant noise of explosions, and from the whistling and falling of balls. The fury of the storm had scarcely abated, when the tumult and din of the Federal batteries and musketry recommenced; and far from the rain extinguishing the fuse of the shell, there seemed to be an un- usually large number falling this morning. I began to feel thoroughly thawed and revived when

George set the breakfast on the table and M—— came in; so we sat down quite gayly, in spite of the continued falling of the rain.

The pleasant fire was doing its work, and the earth, was rapidly hardening around us.

M—— told me of a colonel of one of the regiments stationed at the foot of one of the fortified hills, who unfortunately slept too long, and the turbulent rush of the waters down the hill broke through all barriers, enveloping him completely in mud, water, sand, and sediment. He sprang from the ground in a towering rage, and could scarcely be persuaded that he was not the victim of a practical joke. So soundly had he slept, that he was entirely oblivious of the storm, and could scarcely believe his rude awakening the work of the elements. M—— told me also, with a grave face, of the poor soldiers he had seen in the rifle pits that morning, standing in water—some with little pieces of carpet drawn around them; others with nothing but their thin clothes, which were saturated; and there they would lie through the day, with only the meal of yesterday to sustain them.

CHAPTER 21

Weary

I am told by my friends, who call, that I am looking worn and pale, and frequently asked if I am not weary of this cave life. I parry the question as well as possible, for I do not like to admit it for M——'s sake; yet, I *am* tired and weary—ah! so weary! I never was made to exist under ground; and when I am obliged to, what wonder that I vegetate, like other unfortunate plants—grow wan, spindling, and white! yet, I must reason with myself: I had chosen this life of suffering with one I love; and what suffering, after all, have I experienced?—privations in the way of good and wholesome food, not half what the poor people around us are experiencing.

A fear of those that can kill the body, and after that have no more that they can do! I will not be unnerved—I have no right to complain. *Wherever He hath placed me, there will I be found in His strength*; and hereafter I will be brave and steadfast.

To reason with myself in this time of danger was one of the chief employments of my cave life. Time passes on, and all say the siege cannot last much longer; and still we are here—and still the deafening noise of shells—and the variety of missiles that are thrown fall, scattering death in all directions.

About this time, the town was aroused by the arrival of a courier from General Johnston, who brought private despatches to General Pemberton, the nature of which did not transpire; yet, from the very silence of General Pemberton, the officers augured the worst.

The courier brought many letters to the inhabitants from friends without. His manner of entering the city was singular: Taking a skiff in the Yazoo, he proceeded to its confluence with the Mississippi, where he tied the little boat, entered the woods, and awaited the night. At dark he took off his clothing, placed his despatches securely within them, bound the package firmly to a plank, and, going into the river, he sustained his head above the water by holding to the plank, and, in this manner, floated in the darkness through the fleet, and on two miles down the river to Vicksburg, where his arrival was hailed as an event of great importance, in the still life of the city.

The hill opposite our cave might be called "death's point" from the number of animals that had been killed in eating the grass on the sides and summit. In all directions I can see the turf turned up, from the shells that have gone ploughing into the earth. Horses or mules that are tempted to mount the hill by the promise of grass that grows profusely there, invariably come limping down wounded, to die at the base, or are brought down dead from the summit.

A certain number of mules are killed each day by the commissaries, and are issued to the men, all of whom prefer the fresh meat, though it be of mule, to the bacon and salt rations that they have eaten for so long a time without change. There have already been some cases of scurvy: the soldiers have a horror of the disease; therefore, I suppose, the mule meat is all the more welcome. Indeed, I petitioned M——— to have some served on our table. He said: "No; wait a little longer." He did not like to see me eating mule until I was obliged to; that he trusted Providence would send us some change shortly.

That very afternoon I was looking out on the opposite hill, where the shells were falling frequently. I noticed a very large, fine cow slowly grazing on the side, and ascending higher and higher as she moved.

It was a matter of wonder with me where she came from, for beef cattle of all kinds had disappeared from Vicksburg. The cow was in fine condition; and I thought: Poor creature, you are not prudent in eating such dangerous grass. A short time before tea, M——— came up laughing, and said: "Providence has indeed sent you fresh meat, so that you will not have to depend upon mule. A fine cow has been killed by a shell on the opposite hill. The general has taken the meat, and a large share has been sent to you."

I regretted the fate of the animal that I had so lately seen vigorous with life; yet now, "since fate was so unkind," I gladly received my portion, thinking of the old saw, "*it's an ill wind*," &c. George and some of the boys in the camp cut the meat in strips; and I was able to send some soup meat to the courier that rode continually among the shower of balls, and to a poor humped-back soldier, whose strength was giving way from the privation he had undergone: the remainder was rubbed with saltpetre, strung on canes laid across frames, with a slow fire underneath; and the heat of the sun and the fire combined jerked it nicely for future use.

I laughed heartily at the appearance of the cave a day or two after the process. The logs of the roof were hung with festoons of jerked meat, that swung gracefully and constantly above us; and walking around under it, I felt, quite like an Indian, I suppose, after a successful chase, that starvation for a while was far in the background.

It was astonishing how the young officers kept up their spirits, frequently singing quartets and glees amid the pattering of Minié balls; and I often heard gay peals of laughter from headquarters, as the officers that had spent the day, and perhaps the night, previous in the rifle pits, would collect to make out reports. This evening a gentleman visited us, and, among other songs, sang words to the air of the "*Mocking Bird*," which I will write:

> *'Twas at the siege of Vicksburg,*
> *Of Vicksburg, of Vicksburg—*
> *'Twas at the siege of Vicksburg,*
> *When the Parrott shells were whistling through the air*
> *Listen to the Parrott shells—*
> *Listen to the Parrott shells:*
> *The Parrott shells are whistling through the air.*
>
> *Oh! well will we remember—*
> *Remember—remember*
> *Tough mule meat, June sans November,*
> *And the Minié balls that whistled through the air.*
> *Listen to the Minié balls—*
> *Listen to the Minié balls:*
> *The Minié balls are singing in the air.*

Songs of every description are composed in honour of narrow escapes, unlucky incidents, brave deeds, &c,; songs—humorous, pathetic, and tragic—are sung in every manner of voice. Sometimes hoarse, with surprising loudness and depth; again, with richly modulated tones and much soft volume and melody—all sing, according to differently accustomed tastes.

I heard, one night, a soldier down the ravine singing one of the weird, melodious hymns that negroes often sing; and, amid the firing and crashing of projectiles, it floated up to me in soft, musical undertones that were fascinating in the extreme: the wailing of the earthly unrest— the longing for the glorious home that the warm imagery pictures to be glorious in golden lights and silvery radiance—of song and brilliant happiness! The voice was full and triumphant. Then the rapid change, in low and mournful cadence, to the earth, the clay, the mire—to dearth, to suffering, to sin! "I wonder, Lord, will I ever get to heaven—to the New Jerusalem?" came with the ending of every verse. I bowed my face in my hands. Yes! heaven was so far off! Yet— "*he that Cometh to me, I will in nowise cast out*" our grasp is firm, but our eyes are blind. Some day, after the earthly longings are stilled, we will know the exceeding glory.

Though singing songs of every description, yet how often we are made to feel that any moment the summons may come!

I was sewing, one day, near one side of the cave, where the bank slopes and lights up the room like a window. Near this opening I was sitting, when I suddenly remembered some little article I wished in another part of the room. Crossing to procure it, I was returning, when a Minié ball came whizzing through the opening, passed my chair, and fell beyond it. Had I been still sitting, I should have stopped it. Conceive how speedily I took the chair into another part of the room, and sat in it!

CHAPTER 22

A Wounded Horse

One evening I noticed one of the horses tied in the ravine, acting very strangely—writhing and struggling as if in pain. One of the soldiers went to him and found that he was very badly wounded in the flank by a Minié ball. The poor creature's agony was dreadful: he would reach his head up as far as possible into the tree to which he was tied, and cling with his mouth, while his neck and body quivered with the pain. Every motion, instead of being violent, as most horses would have been when wounded, had a stately grace of eloquent suffering that is indescribable. How I wanted to go to him and pat and soothe him! The halter was taken off, and he was turned free. Going to a tree, he leaned his body against it, and moaned, with half closed eyes, shivering frequently throughout his huge body, as if the pain were too great to bear.

Then, turning his head entirely around, he would gaze at the group of soldiers that stood pityingly near, as if he was looking for human sympathy. The master refused to have him shot, hoping he would recover; but it must have been evident that this day was the last of his strong, proud life: the noble black was doomed. After the gentle faithfulness of his service, it was cruel to prolong his suffering: after the simple meals of mulberry leaves, with scarcely sustenance enough to maintain life, why should this pain and agony be permitted to rack his already weakened body? These truths were set aside, and the master looked with pity; yet, it seemed, a selfish pity.

Becoming restless with the pain, the poor brute staggered blindly on. And now my eyes fill with tears; for he has fallen, with a weary moan, between the banks of the little rivulet in the ravine, his head thrown on the sod, and the bright, intelligent eye turned still upon the men who have been his comrades in many a battle, standing still

75

near him.

Poor fellow!—those low and frequent moans and trembling limbs tell them that death has stricken you already—that you are far beyond human sympathy. In the midst of all the falling shells, cannot one reach him, giving him peace and death? I see an axe handed to one of the bystanders, and turn suddenly away from the scene. The quick, soft stroke! I know it must be over. Again I look, and the glossy, black body is being taken out from our sight, to be replaced by new sufferings, and to be forgotten in new incidents.

There is one missile, were I a soldier, that would totally put me to rout—and that is a shrapnel shell. Only those who have heard several coming at a time, exploding near, and scattering hundreds of small balls around them, can tell how fearful the noise they make—a wild scream—a clattering and whizzing sound that never fails in striking terror to my heart! It seemed sometimes that as many as fifty balls fell immediately around our door. I could have sent out at any time, near the entrance of our cave, and had a bucketful of balls from shrapnel and the Minié rifle, picked up in the shortest possible time.

One old, gray-headed, cheerful-hearted soldier, whom I had talked with, often, was passing through the ravine for water, immediately opposite our cave. A Minié ball struck him in the lower part of the leg; he coolly stooped down, tied his handkerchief around it, and passed on. So constantly fell projectiles of all descriptions, that I became almost indifferent to them. Only the hideous noise of numerous shrapnel could startle me now. Generally at four o'clock in the morning the shrapnel were thrown more furiously than at any other time through the day. At about seven, the Minié balls began falling, accompanied by Parrott, canister, solid shot, and shrapnel shells; and through every minute in the day this constant play of artillery and musketry was kept up from the Federal lines. General Pemberton had ordered the Confederate batteries to remain silent, Unless particular orders were given to fire, or an assault was made on the works.

One afternoon I remember so vividly! One of the surgeons of the staff was chatting with M——, when I heard a rushing and peculiar sound, as if someone were rapidly cutting through the air, near and around me, with a sword.

Both, the doctor and M—— sprang to their feet, as the sound grew more confused, seeming as if the sudden rush, of a volume of water was pouring down the hill. I saw M——turn to the doctor and say: "They're coming!" I dared not ask any questions; yet, I at first supposed the intrenchments were taken. M——, without a word, drew on another coat and threw the linen one he had worn to me, with a laugh. I suppose I must have looked rather wild; for I could not tell or imagine the meaning of the confusing and singular noise around us. Taking his sword, M—— started immediately. I feared every moment that he would fall, for the balls fell like hail. I turned to the doctor, questioning: "Are they coming over the hill?" He laughed, and said:

"Oh! no; they are only making a charge on the intrenchments; and the rushing in the air you hear is the numerous small balls flying over us."

The strange, bewildering sound lasted for some time. The doctor soon took his leave, saying that the wounded would be brought in for him to attend. I sat for half an hour hearing the constant rushing and surging around me, and the quick dropping of balls; the ground trembled from the frequent discharge of the Confederate cannon. What was likely to be the result, I could not tell; for the ravine below, lately so full of animation, seemed to be totally deserted, save now and then the rapid gallop of a courier through the shower of balls along the road. Soon there came a gradual cessation, quieting more and more down to the old interval of a minute between the discharges; soon M came home, reporting one or two wounded and one killed. It seems miraculous to me that, amid such a shower of balls, so few persons should be injured.

CHAPTER 23

An Unhappy Accident

A few days after the assault on the Confederate fortifications, a sad accident cast a gloom over all the little community encamped in the ravine—officers, soldiers, and servants: A soldier, named Henry, had noticed my little girl often, bringing her flowers at one time, an apple at another, and again a young mocking bird, and had attached her to him much by these little kindnesses. Frequently, on seeing him pass, she would call his name, and clap her hands gleefully, as he rode the general's handsome horse for water, causing him to prance past the cave for her amusement. She called my attention to him one morning, saying: "O mamma, look at Henny's horse how he plays!" He was riding a small black horse that was exceedingly wild, and striving to accustom it to the rapid evolutions of the Texas troops, turning in his saddle to grasp something from the ground, as he moved speedily on. Soon after, he rode the horse for water; and I saw him return and fasten it to a tree.

Afterward I saw him come down the hill opposite, with an unexploded shrapnel shell in his hand. In a few moments I heard a quick explosion in the ravine, followed by a cry—a sudden, agonized cry. I ran to the entrance, and saw a courier, whom I had noticed frequently passing by, roll slowly over into the rivulet of the ravine and lie motionless, at a little distance: Henry—oh, poor Henry!—holding out his mangled arms—the hands torn and hanging from the bleeding, ghastly wrists—a fearful wound in his head—the blood pouring from his wounds. Shot, gasping, wild, he staggered around, crying piteously, "Where are you, boys? O boys, where are you? Oh, I am hurt! I am hurt! Boys, come to me!—come to me! God have mercy! Almighty God, have mercy!"

My little girl clung to my dress, saying, "O mamma, poor Henny's killed! Now he'll die, mamma. Oh, poor Henny!" I carried her away from the painful sight.

My first impulse was to run down to them with the few remedies I possessed. Then I thought of the crowd of soldiers around the men; and if M—— should come and see me there—the only lady—he might think I did wrong; so I sent my servant, with camphor and other slight remedies I possessed, and turned into my cave, with a sickened heart.

In a few moments, the litters pass by, going toward the hospital, the blood streaming from that of Henry, who still moaned and cried "for the boys to come to him," and "for God to pity him."

But the other bore the still, motionless body of the young courier, who, in the strength of his life, had been so suddenly stricken. It seems that the two men had been trying to take out the screw from an un-exploded shell for the purpose of securing the powder; in turning it, the fuse had become ignited, communicating the fire to the powder, and the fatal explosion ensued.

Henry had been struck in the head by a fragment—his hands torn from his arms; one or two fragments had also lodged in his body. The courier had been struck in two places in his head, and a number of balls had entered his body. Poor soldier! his mother lived in Yazoo City; and he was her only son. So near was she, yet unable to hold his head and set the seal of her love on his lips ere the breath fled from them forever! He lived until the sun went down, speaking no word—making no moan; only the quickly drawn breath told that life still flickered in the mangled body. Henry died, also, that night, still unconscious of the sorrowful comrades around his bed—still calling on God to pity him.

After the bodies of the wounded men had been carried away, we heard loud wailings and cries in the direction of the city. I was told a negro woman, in walking through the yard, had been struck by a fragment of shell, and instantly killed. The screams of the women of Vicksburg were the saddest I have ever heard. The wailings over the dead seemed full of a heart-sick agony. I cannot attempt to describe the thrill of pity, mingled with fear, that pierced my soul, as suddenly vibrating through the air would come these sorrowful shrieks!—these pitiful moans!—sometimes almost simultaneously with the explosion of a shell. This anguish over the dead and wounded was particularly low and mournful, perhaps from the depression. Many women were utterly sick through constant fear and apprehension. It is strange that the ladies were almost constantly in caves, and yet, did one go out for a short time, she was almost certain to be wounded; while the officers and soldiers rode and walked about, with very little destruction of life ensuing.

An officer was telling me of two soldiers near his camp, who had been severely wounded by Minié balls—one shot through the hand and lung; the other through the side.

A new cause for apprehension came to me about this time: the mortar boats were endeavouring to throw their bombs as far as the intrenchments, and almost succeeded. I could see them at night falling near the opposite hill; and I was in a constant state of trepidation, lest they should be cast still nearer us. After witnessing the brilliant streams of light that they created in the heavens, one night, and feeling repeatedly thankful that they always fell short of the hill we inhabited, I gradually grew sleepy in utter loneliness, for M—— seldom finished receiving reports until eleven. I wearily turned to the little mattress on the floor, said my prayers, and retired.

I had been sleeping some time, for the moon was shining brightly, when I was awakened by loud cries and screams: "Where shall we go? Oh! where shall we go?" My immediate conclusion was that some woman had been killed or wounded, as every now and then I could see the mortar shells dropping on the hill opposite. I therefore thought that I had been spared in Vicksburg, as long as I reasonably could hope, from the variety of changes through which I had passed; and immediately I was seized with a severe panic. If shells had not been falling from the battlefield also, I fear I should have started in that direction— so great was my dread of the mortars!—and run, I cared not where, out of their range.

But the counter awe of Parrott shells kept me where I was. I sat up in bed in a fearful state of excitement; called M—— again and again, without the slightest response; at last, a sleepily uttered "What is the matter?" gave me an opportunity of informing him that we would all be killed, and telling him, while the cold moisture of fear broke out over my forehead, that the mortar shells were nearer than ever, and that the next one would probably fall upon our cave.

Awakened at last to my distressed state of mind, and hearing me say that I knew some woman had been killed, he got up, dressed, took up his cap, and went out to see what had happened, telling me he would return shortly—looking back, laughing as he went, and saying to me that I was fearfully demoralized for so good a soldier. He soon returned, telling me that a negro man had been killed at the entrance of a cave a little beyond us, toward the city; that his mistress, wife, and the young ladies of the family were very badly frightened, having taken refuge in the adjutant's office.

Chapter 24

Death of a Faithful Servant

The next day, the family were invited up to our cave; and the lady told me, with tears, of the death of the faithful old man, who had served her mother before her. The morning of the day he died, he called her to him, and said: "Mistess, I feel like I ain't gwin' to live much longer. Tell young master, when you see him, that I've been praying for him dis day; tell him it smites my heart mightily to think I won't see his young face dis day with the childern. Please tell the young folks, mistess, to come; and let me pray with them."

"Oh! uncle!" the mistress answered, "don't talk that way; you will live many years yet, I hope."

The young ladies were called, and knelt, while he prayed for them and all he loved, shaking hands with them, and speaking to each one separately, as they left. His cave was next his mistress's. That night he sat smoking his pipe near the entrance, when a mortar shell, exploding near, sent a fragment into the old man's side, rending it open, and tearing away his hip. He lived a few moments, and was carried into the cave. Turning to his mistress, while he shook his head, he said: "Don't stay here, mistess. I said the Lord wanted me." And so the good old Christian died. When he had breathed his last, a sudden panic seized them, for shell after shell fell near them; and they all ran. Some of the gentlemen, hearing them cry, brought them to headquarters.

The next day, the news came that one of the forts to the left of us had been undermined and blown up, killing sixty men; then of the death of the gallant Colonel Irwin, of Missouri; and again, the next day, of the death of the brave old General Green, of Missouri.

We were now swiftly nearing the end of our siege life: the rations had nearly all been given out. For the last few days I had been sick; still I tried to overcome the languid feeling of utter prostration. My little one had swung in her hammock, reduced in strength, with a low fever flushing in her face. M—— was all anxiety, I could plainly see. A soldier brought up, one morning, a little jaybird, as a plaything for the child. After playing with it for a short time, she turned wearily away. "Miss Mary," said the servant, "she's hungry; let me make her some soup from the bird." At first I refused: the poor little plaything should not die; then, as I thought of the child, I half consented. With the utmost haste, Cinth disappeared; and the next time she appeared, it was with a cup of soup, and a little plate, on which lay the white meat of the poor little bird.

On Saturday a painful calm prevailed: there had been a truce proclaimed; and so long had the constant firing been kept up, that the stillness now was absolutely oppressive.

At ten o'clock General Bowen passed by, dressed in full uniform, accompanied by Colonel Montgomery, and preceded by a courier bearing a white flag. M—— came by, and asked me if I would like to walk out; so I put on my bonnet and sullied forth beyond the terrace, for the first time since I entered. On the hill above us, the earth was literally covered with fragments of shell—Parrott, shrapnel, canister; besides lead in all shapes and forms, and a long kind of solid shot, shaped like a small Parrott shell. Minié balls lay in every direction, flattened, dented, and bent from the contact with trees and pieces of wood in their flight. The grass seemed deadened—the ground ploughed into furrows in many places; while scattered over all, like giants' pepper, in numberless quantity, were the shrapnel balls.

I could now see how very near to the rifle pits my cave lay: only a small ravine between the two hills separated us. In about two hours. General Bowen returned. No one knew, or seemed to know, why a truce had been made; but all believed that a treaty of surrender was pending. Nothing was talked about among the officers but the all-engrossing theme. Many wished to cut their way out and make the risk their own; but I secretly hoped that no such bloody hazard would be attempted.

The next morning, M—— came up, with a pale face, saying: "It's all over! The white flag floats from our forts! Vicksburg has surrendered!"

He put on his uniform coat, silently buckled on his sword, and prepared to take out the men, to deliver up their arms in front of the fortification.

I felt a strange unrest, the quiet of the day was so unnatural. I walked up and down the cave until M—— returned. The day was extremely warm; and he came with a violent headache. He told me that the Federal troops had acted splendidly; they were stationed opposite the place where the Confederate troops marched up and stacked their arms; and they seemed to feel sorry for the poor fellows who had defended the place for so long a time. Far different from what he had expected, not a jeer or taunt came from any one of the Federal soldiers. Occasionally, a cheer would be heard; but the majority seemed to regard the poor unsuccessful soldiers with a generous sympathy.

After the surrender, the old gray-headed soldier, in passing on the hill near the cave, stopped, and, touching his hat, said:

"It's a sad day this, madam; I little thought we'd come to it, when we first stopped in the intrenchments. I hope you'll yet be happy, madam, after all the trouble you've seen,"

To which I mentally responded, "Amen." The poor, hunchback soldier, who had been sick, and who, at home in Southern Missouri, is worth a million of dollars, I have been told, yet within Vicksburg has been nearly starved, walked out today in the pleasant air, for the first time for many days,

I stood in the doorway and caught my first sight of the Federal uniform since the surrender. That afternoon the road was filled with them, walking about, looking at the forts and the headquarter horses: wagons also filled the road, drawn by the handsome United States horses. Poor M——, after keeping his horse upon mulberry leaves during the forty-eight days, saw him no more! After the surrender in the evening, George rode into the city on his mule: thinking to "shine," as the negroes say, he rode M——'s handsome, silver-mounted dragoon-saddle. I could not help laughing when he returned, with a sorry face, reporting himself safe, but the saddle gone.

M—— questioned and requestioned him, aghast at his loss; for a saddle was a valuable article in our little community; and George, who felt as badly as anyone, said: "I met a Yankee, who told me: 'Git down oif dat mule; I'm gwin' to tab dat saddle.' I said: 'No; I ain't gwin' to do no such thing.' He took out his pistol, and I jumped down."

So Mister George brought back to M—— a saddle that better befitted his mule than the one he rode off on—a much worn, common affair, made of wood. I felt sorry for M——. That evening George brought evil news again: another horse had been taken. His remaining horse and his only saddle finished the news of the day.

The next morning, Monday, as I was passing through the cave, I saw something stirring at the base of one of the supports of the roof: taking a second look, I beheld a large snake curled between the earth and the upright post. I went out quickly and sent one of the servants for M——, who, coming up immediately, took up his sword and fastened one of the folds of the reptile to the post. It gave one quick dart toward him, with open jaws. Fortunately, the length of the sword was greater than the upper length of body; and the snake fell to the earth, a few inches from M—— who set his heel firmly on it, and severed the head from the body with the sword. I have never seen so large a snake; it was fully as large round the body as the bowl of a good-sized glass tumbler, and over two yards long.

CHAPTER 25

George My Protector

In the afternoon, M—— went into the city, with some of the officers, to make arrangements for me. I was much amused, though I did not let them see it, as they set off on their poor mulberry-fed horses. M—— had been presented by someone, after the loss of his horse, with a little, lame, subdued-looking animal, to whom food of any kind seemed a rarity; and the poor horse ambled along as if he considered his weight a great affliction. Our whole little household had been drawn out to witness the departure of the brilliant (?) cavalcade.

Afterward, as I sat with a book at the entrance, I heard steps, and, looking up, I saw a large, burly negro, with a most disagreeable face, dressed in Federal uniform, and armed, coming up the little path that led to the cave. As he advanced toward me, I sprang to my feet; but George, who was luckily near, crossed over from the "*sassafras* bed," carving knife in hand, with which he was digging some of the root. Standing between us, he said: "Where are yon gwin', old man?"

"None your business," he returned, pausing a moment. I was just on the point of calling for some of the gentlemen at headquarters, when he turned and went round the cave on the hill.

"I'll make dis knife show you what's your business," growled George. Poor George! he had been my faithful defender throughout all my vicissitudes in Vicksburg.

Soon after, George came to me in a great state of excitement, and said: "Oh! Miss Mary, a Yankee soldier was just going with our tent fly from the top of the cave, and I made him stop and leave it." A Federal soldier came down the side of the hill, stopped, and took my little daughter's hand and said some pleasant words to her; turned to me, touching his hat, with a smile, and said, "Good morning." I bowed in return, while a lucky thought came to me: Here was a kind-hearted,

86

polite soldier; why not let him take the tent fly, in the place of some undeserving man?

So I said: "Soldier, would you like a tent fly?"

He answered: "Oh! yes, madam; I would like one very much."

So I sent George to get it for him. He expressed himself very grateful—disliked to take it, fearful of robbing us; but I assured him he was welcome; so he again bade me good morning, and carried off his acquisition.

The Confederate troops were being marched into Vicksburg to take the parole that the terms of the treaty of surrender demanded. In a few days they would leave the city they had held so long.

On Friday they began their march toward the South; and on Saturday poor George came to me, and said he had put on a pair of blue pants, and, thinking they would take him for a Federal soldier, had tried to slip through after M—— but he was turned back; so he came, begging me to try and get him a pass: the effort was made; and to this day I do not know whether he ever reached M—— or not.

Saturday evening, Vicksburg, with her terraced hills—with her pleasant homes and sad memories, passed from my view in the gathering twilight—passed, but the river flowed on the same, and the stars shone out with the same calm light! But the many eyes—O Vicksburg!—that have gazed on thy terraced hills—on thy green and sunny gardens—on the flow of the river—the calm of the stars—those eyes! how many thou hast closed on the world forever!

Letters of Trial and Travel

My dear J——:

I am just in from dinner; and you would be amused to see the different faces—I might as well say the different appetites; for the Army of Missouri and Arkansas have been undergoing rigorous fasts of late; and the little episode of the Battle of Elkhorn and the consequent privations have helped not a little the gaunt appearance of these military characters. All eat, eat rapidly; from General V—— D—— down to the smallest lieutenant, whose manner of playing the epicure over the different dishes ordered, is a study. The confidential consultations with the waiter over them, together with the knowing unconsciousness of bestowing his small change, almost convinces me that he is a brigadier-general, or a colonel, at least. You see streaming in constantly this tide of human beings, to eat, stare at the ladies, talk, and order much wine in the excitement of military anecdotes; for you must understand that a civilian is a "*rara avis*" amid the brilliant uniforms of the dining room. Yet, amid all this mass and huge crowd, the majority are polished gentlemen, who have evidently seen much of the world, and who are men of purpose and character.

General V—— D——and staff sit not far from me—looked at rather jealously by the Missourians, as ranking and commanding them over their favourite general. Yet, he always treats the old general with the utmost consideration and courtesy. On the other side sits General P——, with his kind, benevolent face. The poor old gentleman finds at the table his lightest reserves become his heaviest forces: nearly all his staff are about him.

And, as I sit half amused at the expression of some faces, and thinking deeply of the mute, yet determined impress of character on others, two gentlemen come in—one in plain citizen's clothing, with heavy black beard and high forehead—with stooping gait and hands behind him. I am told he is Governor J——, of Missouri. His face puzzles me—it is thoughtful and singular. By his side, with tall, lithe, slender figure, fully erect, walks General J—— T——. You will scarcely think it possible that this is the so-frequently talked of J—— T——.

I thought him an ordinary man, did not you? Yet, this is anything but an ordinary man. The keen dark eye sweeps the room as he enters, taking us all in at a glance—a quick, daring, decisive, resolute face, I can make nothing more out of him. Yet, there is more of thought and intellect than you see at first. He is dressed in full uniform, with sword and sash, and has quite a military air.

There are many Saint Louisians here; you see them scattered around the tables quite plentifully. General C—— is among the number. He sits at some distance, and looks quite worn and sad. You know—do you not?—that he is the father of young Churchill Clark, who was killed at Elkhorn. Have I ever told you his history? It is this: He graduated at West Point in the commencement of the war; and knowing and having a great admiration for General P——, he joined him at once: he was put in command of some artillery; and showing himself a youth of courage and ability—for he was only twenty years old—his command was increased. Throughout the constant trials and sufferings of the campaign, he showed himself equal in courage, daring, and judgment, to many older heads. He was particularly beloved by General P——. At Elkhorn, as ever, his battery sustained itself with coolness and bravery. As the general rode by, he said some cheering words to young Clark, who took off his cap and waved it, saying, "General, we will hold our own," or words to that effect, when a ball sped from the enemy, and crashed in the young, ardent brain as he spoke.

I have been told that the general was affected to tears. He knelt by his side, vainly seeking for some trace of the strong, young life, but the pulses were stilled forever; and Churchill Clark lay a stiffened corpse in the long, wet grass at Elkhorn. And so his father sits silent and alone, and all respect the grief that none can assuage.

In a few days we leave. The gentlemen all go to Corinth, where a battle, in all probability, will take place before long. Fort Pillow can hardly hold out, under the daily bombardment that we hear from the gunboats; and if it falls, Memphis, on taking leave of the Confederate officers, will usher in the Federal to quarters in the Gayoso.   *Adieu.*

Memphis, April.

Dear J——:

Again I write you from the Gayoso House, which still teems with Missourians, and many ladies—some few from St. Louis. General P——'s parlour is filled with ladies from morning until night. I have been told that on one occasion some ladies, who were the reverse of beautiful, were coming in to see him, when he turned to one of his staff officers, and told him that it was his duty to assist him—that here was an opportunity: he must kiss these ladies for him; but the officer was politely deaf until too late.

It is astonishing to see how ladies do flock to see the old general; and all kiss him, as a matter of course. I rode out to the camp of the Missourians with M——, a few mornings since. It is pleasantly situated near the bank of the river. The men seem to be in good spirits; although moving them across the Mississippi has been an unpopular act. The poor fellows are being taken out to Corinth as fast as transportation can be furnished them. The compliment is paid them of being placed in the most dangerous position; for we daily expect an attack from the Federal forces on Corinth.

Would you like to see those you love complimented in this way? You can form no idea of the love and devotion shown by the Missouri troops for their general. I happened to be standing near a window at the end of the hall, last evening, as some regiments passed by the Gayoso on their way out to the depot, bound for Corinth.

General P—— stood out on the veranda as they passed by, and shouts and cheers for the old general and Missouri rent the air. General J—— T—— called on me this morning, and amused me much with some of his adventures in Missouri last winter; among others, he told us of his dash into the little town of Commerce for food. His men were ordered to take a certain amount, lay down the money, and leave. As he sat on a small horse, waiting for them, out came the "heroine of Commerce," as he called the lady. I have forgotten her name; yet, I think it was O'Sullivan.

She walked up to the general, shook her clenched hand in his face, and told him he was a robber and a scoundrel. Her husband pulled her by the arm and tried to make her desist; but she was deaf to his entreaties, standing part of the time on one side of the little horse, and part of the time on the other; first, shaking her clenched hand at him, and then standing, with arms folded, calling him all manner of names. Some of the officers wished General T—— to have her confined to her own house until his departure; but he laughed, and said: "No; let her alone." She still continued hovering around him, threatening and talking.

He said: "Oh! Mrs, O'Sullivan, you are a modest woman—a very modest woman. Madam, don't you think your house stands in need of you?" Powerless fell the irony: wherever he went, he was followed by the persistent Mrs. O'Sullivan; stop where he would, Mrs. O'Sullivan was by his side, much to the amusement of his followers; go where he would, up rose Mrs. O'Sullivan unexpectedly at corners—red-faced and bitter—always in the same belligerent, defiant state.

A steamboat was seen coming down the river. General T—— ordered his men to hide behind a woodpile until it came up, expecting to get supplies from it. When they thought themselves disposed out of sight. General T—— raised his eyes, and behold! some little distance up the river, stood the inevitable Mrs. O'Sullivan, violently gesticulating to the boat, and crying, "Turn, turn! J—— T—— is here;" at the same time waving her apron and sun bonnet, in quite a frantic manner. The boat turned indeed; and although the scheme failed, behind the woodpile sat General T——, chagrined at the failure, yet laughing most heartily at the attitude and *mal-à-propos* appearance of Mrs. O'Sullivan.

The hotel is crowded with military men: many wounded at the late Battle of Shiloh, going around with arms in slings; others supported by crutches. The ladies are seemingly having a very gay time: the halls are filled with promenaders, and the parlours with gay young couples, music, and laughter.

Yet, a sudden surprise has come to all: New Orleans has fallen—an unexpected blow to most of the Southern officers. I cannot but think, as I see all the life and bustle around me, of the different scenes a week or two hence, when the fearful battle of Corinth will have taken place. How many that are now happy and full of life, looking forward with confidence to the laurels that may be won, before the struggle is over will be silent forever in death! or, worse, perhaps lamed and maimed for life! General Beauregard's works are said to be fine; yet, the Federal approaches are said to be greatly superior.

My husband goes tomorrow to Corinth; and I will go to O———, Miss., to await the result of what all seem to think will be a most bloody struggle. I will write on reaching O———; until then,   farewell.

O———, May 1st.

The expected battle has not yet come off, and I am still awaiting the result; busying myself about many things, visiting and returning visits from my old friends; dividing my time between the world and the hospital, the lights and shades of life. Ah, the shades! My dear J———, you can little imagine how much suffering I have witnessed in the last few weeks—how much, that acts or kind words have no power to mitigate. There have been many wounded brought in from Corinth, many who have died since their arrival, many who will die; but, saddest of all, a young boy, too young to be a soldier, yet possessing all a soldier's spirit. I walked into a ward, one morning, that I had visited the evening before—a ward of very sick patients—and saw an old man sitting by a new cot, fanning a young boy, who lay with flushed face, and burning eyes fixed on the ceiling. As I advanced toward them, the weather-bronzed man stood stiffly erect, making me a quaint, half-awkward, military salute, saying, as he did so, "My boy, ma'am!"

"Is he wounded?" I asked.

He threw back the sheet that covered him, pointed to the stump of a limb amputated near the thigh: "He has gained the cross," he said, while his head grew more erect, as he held back the sheet with the fan, and his eye shot out the grim ghost of a smile.

A proud, iron soldier the man was, I could see. The boy was delirious; so I shall tell you of the man. Refusing to be seated as long as a lady remained standing in the room, he stood stiffly upright at the head of the cot, keeping each fly from the face of the boy with the tenderness of a mother. A limp brown hat was on the side of his head, shading his eyes, that followed me in all parts of the room. A red cord and tassel hung from one side of his hat, and gave him a jaunty air that was quite out of keeping with the quaint stiffness of his manner. After speaking to the sick and wounded soldiers around, asking after their wounds and wants, I returned to the young boy's cot, and heard the old man's story. Don't be weary if I give it to you; he had so much pride in his boy, let that be my extenuation.

"We belong to the Texas Rangers, ma'am, the boy and me; he could ride as well as the rest of them, ma'am, a year ago. When the war broke out, and we practised regularly like, he was the best rider in the company—could pick anything he wanted off the ground as he was going. He's only fourteen, ma'am—a fine-grown lad, indeed. His mother was the likeliest woman I ever seed," with a deprecating bow to me; "he's got her eyes—the finest eyes God ever made, she had, ma'am. She died when quite young like, leaving him to me, a little shaver, and he's been by me ever since. The boys and me tried to overpersuade him out of the army; 'peared like he was too young for such business; but he wouldn't hear to it, not he, ma'am, and here he is," passing his sleeve across his eyes.

"Well, ma'am, so he staid with us; and when we got to Corinth, General Beauregard offered a cross of honour to the ones that showed themselves the best soldiers. So our boys talked a heap about who'd get it; but this boy says nothing. Well, one day we were ordered out to scout, and we came up with the Yankees, and we fit 'em a half hour or so, when I seed this youngster by my side kind adrooping by a tree, but standing his ground. Well, we routed them at last, when I found the boy's leg was all shattered, and he'd kept up like nothing wan't the matter. So when we went back to Corinth, it got noised about like from the soldiers to the officers—how he'd held out.

"And, more'n all, the time when his leg was being cut off, we couldn't get any chloroform, morphine, or the like: he just sit up like a brave lad, and off it went, without a word out of him. So the doctors they talked of that; and he's been notified that he'll get the first cross, and the boys'll be monstrous fond of him, and feel most like they'd got it themselves. If he'd get rid of his fever and pick up like, I'd be a happy man," he said anxiously.

Pardon me do I tire you; but let me take you to visit the sick prisoners. The old man that we pass in the hall, with his arm and leg in a frame, will never recover; yet he does not know it, and frequently asks me if I think he will get a pension when he is well, if he loses his leg and arm. He persists in keeping his face covered with a handkerchief, raising it up and peeping out, if he hears my voice, each day, with his usual salutation: "You've come, have ye?" If I bring any little article of food that I think the patients will relish, this old man must be fed by me, and I am frequently amused at the directions he gives me, for he is extremely practical and particular: "Now, if you will turn the spoon a little to one side, I will turn my mouth in this direction, and the custard will pass safely in." Poor man, without a friend, both arms badly wounded, and leg shattered, dying by degrees, yet to the last the handkerchief would be raised, and the cheery welcome greet me, "Ye're come, have ye?"

I think I can see you looking around in this ward to learn which are the prisoners, for all seem cheerful and talkative. In this cot by the door, with a wounded limb in a frame—like a huge lion—lies a man, large whiskered, large bodied, and long limbed, yet with a pleasant smile of greeting as we enter and make our inquiries after his wound. He is "better this morning, thank you," or, "I am obliged to you, not quite so well." A little picture on the table by his side, of a child three years of age, is never closed. A little child, blue eyed, with bare white neck, and plump round arms, showing the mother's wish that the picture should be fair and lovely to the father's eye. The Federal flag is on the cover.

The man, a captain, is of an Illinois company. The child and mother, with tearful eyes and wistful hearts, look over the wide expanse of land and water that separates, over the cruel bounds that man has set—still faithful in their love. Still watching, and hoping, for the time when liberty will be his, and he, constant and true, will return to them. He tells me the name of the little one, with a sorrowful look at me with his dark eye. If he is free, if he ever sees these words, he will remember how the little one was gazed on by a lady in deep mourning, to whose heart a child of three years brought a sad and tearful memory.

Come to the next cot with me; do not shrink from this blackened brow. Yesterday this was a noble-faced, gray-haired, old Confederate soldier, with the plaintive, lovely smile of perfect resignation. He suffers much from a wound in his body; seldom talks, yet always smiles gratefully for the slightest attention. This morning I find the erysipelas has broken out, spreading over his forehead and a part of his face. He cautions me, with the same pleasant, resigned smile, about coming near him, lest I take the disease. The blackened skin is from the effect of iodine to stay its progress. He will not live: dear, patient old man, my heart aches for him, yet I can give him nothing but kind words.

This morning I brought the men in this ward toast. The old man slept, and I gave to each his portion. Engaged in talking to a prisoner in another part of the room, I heard the Illinoisan say: "Let me divide this toast with you; I do not need it all."

I turned, and heard the old man reply: "Oh, no; you keep it." I procured his toast and brought it to him, laughingly telling the prisoner I believed I saw the dawn of the millennium.

Do you not wish, dear J——, that the dawning was indeed with us; that brave and noble men should no more suffer, bleed, and die, but live; and in their lives grow more thankful and worthy of the Divine blood that has been shed for the removal of the fearful suffering and warfare that is all around us?

Pardon me for the length of time I have detained you, and remember me as ever, dear J——,

Yours.

O——, June, 1862.

Can you credit it, dear J——, General Beauregard has evacuated Corinth? you have learned it by this time through the papers, and share with me the surprise. Our feelings have fluctuated with the news from Corinth for weeks. First, an engagement would probably ensue the following day. Then, someone had heard heavy guns, and was sure that the battle had taken place. And the next day, all quiet at Corinth. But the most astonishing of all, for we were prepared for everything besides, Corinth has been left quietly; absolutely left, and the Federal troops probably occupy the place. Everyone has something to say on the subject, and all are more brilliant in their ideas for the reason that all have full scope to exercise them. No one possesses reliable information, and we are a conjecturing community—gentlemen as well as ladies. Something out of the common order of affairs, you will say.

But a truce to politics, of which I am very fond, and, like most women, know very little about. "Why should a woman of sense care to talk about anything but dress and her servants? So I attended a pleasant little *soirée* a few evenings since, graced by the fair and elegant daughters of General P——, of Tennessee, and the young bride of Jacob J——'s only son, a sweet young girl. All were in full evening dress, though the guests were few.

But a novelty, listen: A young Spanish bride—a brilliant woman—dazzled my eyes for the evening. Conversing only in her beautiful national language, she with animated gestures fascinates and enlightens one readily in relation to her themes. Then she warbles most beautifully, and one can scarcely complain that her higher notes lack in power, as she rises from the instrument, placing her hand on her heart, saying brokenly the only English words she is mistress of: "Oh! pity me, pity!" with an arch reverence to her audience.

I am troubled about our poor hospital patients, the one third of whom you have not met with me, each has a separate individuality that interests me exceedingly. It is feared that the Federal troops will advance on O——, and the patients will be removed to a safer place below. I will be sorry to see them leave, poor fellows. The boy that gained a double cross at Corinth has closed his eyes softly and calmly. Suffering will never disturb him more. He is dead. The old man has gone back to his company with spasms of pain in his heart, of which the world will never know.

Let me tell you of the man's devotion. The boy's fever still raged, with slighter and slighter intervals. The medicine failed to procure the desired effect. The physicians looked anxious as they approached his cot. I wanted to take the old man's hand and tell him of the Friend in heaven, from whom death itself can never separate us; but a foolish fear withheld me. One night the physicians met around the little cot, the old man, as usual when others were near, standing stiffly at the head, yet, with alarmed and burning eyes, intently reading each face. A sad reading, hopeless—the eyes told that, while the hand sought the faintly beating pulse. "Doctor, may I try to save my boy my own way?" said the old man, following the physician into the hall. "Yes, do as you choose with him, only do not give him unnecessary pain."

In the morning a large tub of cold water was taken to the ward and placed by the sick boy's cot; and, to the dismay of the soldiers in the beds around, the boy was lifted out, wounded as he was, by the strong and gentle arms of one in whose eyes he was more precious than the rarest of diamonds and gold. A quick douse, and he was rubbed well, covered closely, and soon slept soundly, the perspiration breaking out profusely for the first time in two days. He was decidedly better, and the proud smile on the father's face was a happy thing to see. Gradually he grew more feeble, the fever returned, and one morning, with an aching heart, I saw the calmness of death in the closed eyes and motionless nostril. Standing at the head of the bed, his hat drawn over his eyes, his arms folded in a stern and patient agony, the father stood watching yet, most faithfully. I cannot express to you the grief that my sympathy brought—the grief, and constantly the words: "Alone! all alone! My boy! oh, my boy!"

The ladies wished to have a large funeral over the brave, young soldier; but the physicians would not consent to having him buried in town, saying that the soldiers were all worthy of attention, and that no distinction could be allowed. So, before he was buried, I went out to the hospital and looked my last on the young, dead face, from which all trace of suffering had fled: only peace and rest now forever!

Pain and anguish were making a deep impress on the face of the man by the head: the drawn lines of watching and suffering were more evident, as with a strained smile, and almost a gasp of pain, he thanked me for the interest I had taken. "Everybody is so kind!" he said. He had gone into town that morning and purchased a little black coat, placing it on the small form. A black velvet vest, white bosom, and the cravat tied over the white, boyish throat, told of the tenderness that shrank not from the coldness of death,

"He's like his mother, ma'am, more than ever, now," he whispered, softly drawing the sheet over the inanimate form; and turning squarely around, with his back to me, I saw him draw again and again his sleeve across his eyes. We are born to this human sorrow; and yet it is an appalling thing to me, You have expressed an interest in these visits to the wounded and dying; therefore I speak.

One more life that hovers over the grave!—one more who has suffered, oh, I cannot express to you how much! A prisoner from Iowa, belonging to the Second Iowa Cavalry, was captured at Farmington, near Corinth, shot through the body so badly, that very little hope was entertained of his recovery: he lingered some weeks, and dwindled from a robust, hearty man, down to a poor emaciated being—seldom talking— never complaining, yet suffering much, I could see.

When I came, one morning, the ward master whispered aside to me that he had been dying through the night. I entered the ward; his eye sought mine, with a wistful look, and brightened as I came near his bed. I smoothed the hair from his forehead, moistened his lips, and then, taking the fly brush, resolved to stay by him to the last. Oh, dear J——! those wistful eyes that followed every motion of mine!—those anxious, dying eyes!

What was the poor mother doing now, of whom he whispered to me? How little she knew that the eyes that were so dear, now were looking their last on the light! Far away from home and friends, among strangers, the soul was swiftly passing out into the great sea of eternity, the bright hopes of which so softly regulate this life-tide of ours!—passing out—passing out, with a lingering look of unfathomable speech, into my face; for my face told him what my lips faltered in doing!

"If I can write to your mother before you are free, what shall I say?"

"You know," he whispered.

"You are very sick, and God may not spare your life; will you say one little prayer after me?" And so a few words were said, that, with long pauses, he whispered after me, almost gasping at the last word. And thus beside him I sat, the gaze from his eyes into mine growing more and more intense. It seemed as if his whole soul was drawn out in unutterable language. At length, the quivering eyelid, the softly fleeting breath, ebbing out—yes, ebbing out so swiftly!

O Father! give this tried soul thy rest, through thy dear Son. Free at last, prisoner! Peace to thy soul! God grant his peace!

My friend, do you dread death? I have seen it come so often as a relief from pain and distress, that I could not but bless it. Do not forget that you asked for these details; and believe, as I wish you always to, in my affection. Yours.

It is long since I have heard from you, dear J———; long since I have written. You will notice that I am again at O——— , Soon after writing my last, the Federal troops took possession of Holly Springs and threatened O———. The hospital patients were removed; and I crossed the country to meet my husband, who was at Tupelo. After spending some time in Pontotoc, I continued on to Tupelo, and for some time remained on a plantation six miles distant. Meantime the Battle of Iuka occurred; and the loss of the brave General Little was deeply felt by the Missourians. The troops returned in dejection. Shortly, they were marched across to Ripley, where a junction was formed with the troops under General V——— D———; and an attack was made on Corinth, in which the troops behaved gallantly, but all to no purpose: a complete repulse it proved; and the army under the two generals narrowly escaped capture.

The wives and families of the officers were, of course, distressed and anxious. Couriers daily came galloping into the town, with the most conflicting reports.

At one time we heard that the Missourians were completely cut to pieces; again, that they were all captured. One of the couriers said he had seen my husband lying in an ambulance as he passed. How much distressed I was, you can imagine. Yet, two days passed wearily along; and still no tidings. The evening of the second day, as I sat in the moonlight on the portico, I heard a vehicle coming down the road with great speed; as it neared the house, I saw that it was an ambulance. My worst fears now took shape and form: M——— wounded, perhaps mortally wounded, I thought; and I ran swiftly down the walk. The driver met me at the gate, telling me that he had been sent with all speed after me—that Tupelo would be evacuated during the night, and my husband had written to the post quartermaster, placing me in his charge. I also had a letter. The quartermaster would take me over the country with the wagon train at daylight in the morning. My husband was well, he answered to my first, earnest inquiry.

It was now nine o'clock; my little daughter was in bed sleeping

99

soundly. The man, a sergeant, who was well known to my husband, had, as yet, not supped; so, while he ate, I gathered my baggage together, wrapped a shawl around my sleeping child, and then, with a hurried goodbye, we drove off, six miles through the woods, through what had been an impassable swamp. Now the gloom of the huge trees brought to my mind all the thrilling tales I had heard of travellers being waylaid in swamps and dense woods. I looked at the shadows on the trunks of trees, and imagined a man skulked in the darkness behind them. The owls were crying mournfully, and the plaintive song of the whippoorwill came to us from the dense recesses of the forest. My servant crept closely to my side, for negroes, in their vivid imaginations, fill the woods at night with phantoms and ghosts of the departed. Frequently, after detailing the events of the recent battle to us, our driver, in the full moonlight, would break the silence with one of the stirring camp airs, whistling loud and shrilly; then my martial and political hopes would rise; but as we would again plunge into the darkness of the rugged cypress trees, where the owl and whippoorwill vied with each other, a silence would again come over us, and I again become a timid, fearful woman.

Soon we saw lights through the trees, then the rows of camp fires, and noise and bustle became the prominent features of the town: cattle were driven through, with many a shout and halloo; wagons were passing rapidly; soldiers were cooking rations at the camp fires—a scene of busy preparation.

We drove to the quartermaster's office, and the gentlemen conducted us in, regretting that they had been obliged to send for me in such a summary manner. The order to move had come at dark; and since then they had been employed constantly, as the town must be evacuated by daylight; for the Federal forces were advancing rapidly.

The house was an unfinished building: one large, long room comprised the second story, with a small portion partitioned off, and dignified by the name of office. To this I, with my servant, was conducted through piles of mule collars, harness, bridles, &c.

Here I was glad to find a little camp cot, on which I laid my child for the first time out of my arms. With many apologies for the poor accommodations they had to offer me, the gentlemen took their leave; and I could hear the quick orders to clerks, drivers, and soldiers, as they recommenced their hurried preparations. I took my knitting and sat by the window. The moon was low in the heavens; yet the tumult continued throughout the town. My child slept peacefully—her father many miles away, yet, I knew, filled with anxiety for our welfare.

At dawn we were on our way. The first night, I slept in Pontotoc at a friend's house. The gentlemen camped out of town about a mile. In the morning, before I had left my room, my friends called and left a message for me with the lady of the house. I was to start as soon as I could, and strive to gain the head of the wagon train, thereby escaping the dust. Our driver was a soldier from Arkansas—a quiet, mild, little man, with very little force. We drove on briskly in the pleasant morning air for two or three hours, and saw nothing of the train: perhaps we were before them.

Presently, we stopped and held a consultation. In every opinion that I expressed in regard to the matter, I found a ready echo from the little man, *pro* and *con*. We had driven perhaps too rapidly: no signs of the wagons could we find. Waiting patiently for a time, a disagreeable foreboding crossed my mind. I had not been told which road to take; there were two: perhaps we were on the wrong one. O—— was forty miles from Pontotoc; we had already gone nine, and could not now return expecting to find our friends.

The only alternative was to drive through to O——, where M—— designed meeting us. So, in answer to the little man's query, "Don't you think we'd better whip up and try to make O—— by night?" I said, "Yes." Clouds began to overspread the sky; and I heard mutterings of thunder in the distance; still the sun shone out fitfully; and I hoped the rain would not fall near us. Driving on with speed, we had proceeded but a few miles, when the unmistakable evidences of a storm, that would soon burst upon us, convinced me that a shelter must be sought; where, it was hard tell, for the road we travelled was almost destitute of houses. I was in despair, as the wind whistled around us, driving in eddies the leaves and dried grass about the ground, and swaying high and low, with a moaning sound, the limbs of the huge forest trees. In my anxiety, I grasped at a straw. I remembered, in travelling this road before, that M—— had pointed out a by road through the woods, that led to Lafayette Springs. The proprietor knew my husband; and I resolved to take a country road that I saw leading in the direction I imagined the Springs to be.

Picture me, J——, if you can, sitting up in the centre of the ambulance, my servant by my side, little J—— between us—the little driver, meek and resigned, turning when I said turn, stopping when I said stop. Taking a strange road, I knew not where, we drew near, at last, a most unpromising-looking cabin, the inhabitants of which filled the door at the sound of wheels—in every variety of size—robed in yellow dresses, surmounted by tangled white heads. The old lady "knew thar was some springs somewhar abouts, and reckoned this road might run thar;" then, resuming her pipe, looked for confirmation of the statement to her eldest daughter, who said: "Yes, she reckoned, the road would take us thar, if we kept 'straight ahead.'"

"Whip the mules," I cried, "and drive rapidly;" for the storm was darkening around us; and the ambulance jingled a chorus through the silent "piny woods." Large drops were now falling; the wind moaned and surged mournfully through the "barren," moaned and swept over the narrow road, whirling the "pine points" as we passed; faster and faster fell the rain. Our heavier clothing, shawls, cloaks, &c., were with the trunks: one light shawl, in which I enveloped my child, was all we possessed in this emergency. The ambulance cover was dotted with bullet holes, through which the rain dropped in cold relentlessness.

The little driver was suffering martyrdom: drawn up as closely as possible, with his blanket around him, the wind driving the rain in sheets between him and the mules, he looked to me in the mist like an inanimate, round, brown ball. Soon, the floor of the ambulance filled so rapidly with water, that he threw his blanket over the top of the conveyance to keep the rain from falling through; then subsiding again, the only sign of life about the little being was the mechanical process of whipping the mules.

A little side road presented itself, leading into the forest, freshly marked with wagon tracks. Hearing the barking of a dog not far distant, I ordered the driver to turn in search of a house. Proceeding a quarter of a mile, we came to another little cabin. Through the rain, the weak voice of the little driver brought to the door a woman, who informed us that Lafayette Springs were three miles on "ahead." Highly elate, the little man turned to me, and, with a glad face, saying, "Very good news," whipped up his mules; and I firmly believe the man was nearsighted; for in two minutes more we would have gone off a precipice that was almost hidden by the tops of trees that grew far below at the base. "Stop!" I cried, as the heads of the mules were almost over the verge of the cliff. The little man meekly asked what he should do. "Back the mules!" I cried; and, after a troublesome detention, we at last turned and found ourselves on the road again.

"We like to had a right smart time thar," said the little man to me.

"We did, indeed," I returned, blandly; for I feared I had hurt the poor man's feelings in speaking so quickly at that critical time. Gladly we reached the Springs through the driving rain, and were pleasantly welcomed. The landlord did all that he could for my comfort.

I had the pleasure of meeting a friend who had met my husband, and who told me much about the recent battle. The next morning, we started early. I determined, although it was a raw, disagreeable morning, to be done with my lonely wanderings. We had gone about four miles, shivering in the dismal mist, when I heard a quick galloping along the road. The curtain of the ambulance was lifted—a blithe good morning in a voice I could not mistake: M—— was riding by our side, asking how on earth we had contrived to wander so far off from our friends. I could answer nothing to this bantering. Corinth, with all its bloody horrors that have been so vividly before my mind, the constant anxiety I had felt, and now my tribulations were ended—M—— in person here to take charge of us! I covered my face and cried like a silly child.

Do not blame me; you have never been lost in the woods in a storm, and felt that the responsibility of every action rested with you. M—— had been sent on business to Pontotoc—had heard of us there and followed, fearing that we might have met with some accident. I will accompany M—— in a few days to Holly Springs, where Generals P——, V—— D——, and L——are intrenching with their forces. As I write, the sunlight fades away; and only the fading crimson light lies across my paper. In closing, let me entreat yon to remember always, as you read, my affection for you,   As ever.

Holly Springs.

You wished me to keep a journal for you, dear J——; but I answered that a journal would be a dull compound of dates, with three lines setting forth the vapidity of most days; and I would rather write events as they passed. You replied that my letters must be voluminous if they were satisfactory. Do you not already repent the remark? I rejoice, if length is pleasing, my letters are satisfactory.

The Battle of Corinth was a bloody failure. Oh the blood that has flowed in this wonderful and most appalling warfare!—the tears and the suffering! Can there be nothing done to assuage the fierce passions of men? Oh! J——, could you see, as I have, the torn and mangled human beings brought from the field of battle, with loud cries to God for death!—for mercy and for death!—you, like me, would ask anxiously, "Can nothing do away with this death?—this anguish? Can no appeal be made by which peace may come to us?" But woman weeps, while man strikes!

Holly Springs, with its white verandahed houses, its pleasant gardens, wide streets, and hospitable homes, is the most pleasant of Southern towns; though crowded and teeming with soldiers and officers.

The inhabitants seem uniting in the efforts to entertain. Generals V—— D——, P——, L——, and T—— have each their respective headquarters in the town. A week ago I attended a review of the troops under Generals L——and T——. They presented a fine appearance: most of them were newly uniformed and renovated from their prison clothing. General V—— D——, who is called the finest horseman in the army, galloped up and down the line on a fleet, beautiful black horse, followed by General P—— on a large bay that galloped heavily and with less speed.

There were many ladies present on horseback, scattered around the field, with generally a gay group of officers surrounding them. Day before yesterday we rode out to a large review of the Missouri troops under General P——. There were spectators from the whole country around: many came up on the cars from a distance. Such imperishable renown have the Missouri troops gained in the late Battle of Corinth, that all are anxious to witness their review, and cheer the brave fellows who have suffered so much. Although, driven back and obliged to retreat, their gallant struggle over two rows of superior fortifications in the face of a galling fire, the Southern people will never forget.

General P—— is greatly beloved by the people also; though the heads of the government are strongly opposed to him. It is natural, of course, that President Davis should suppose a regularly educated military man would be more likely to understand the science of war than a man who had not made it his study. But why does he cripple so efficient an officer as General P—— certainly is, so as almost to render him inefficient?

The Missourians on review looked fresh and lively. General P——, attended by his staff, stood near us in the pause, while we waited the arrival of General V—— D——. One of General P——'s staff officers started across the field to carry a despatch, when his horse, stumbling, fell on the grass, rolling the brilliantly uniformed gentleman over and over on the sod, much to the amusement of the spectators, who cheered him lustily. I felt sorry for him; and although some of his friends were talking to me at the time, I could scarcely conceal a smile. But the men, who, half a mile distant, have been drawn in line, now wheel, form, and march around the little hillock in the distance. See, the sun glances on the bayonets of the guns, as they ascend, and in coming down over the brow of the hill, the regular swing of the line and glance of the steel show the discipline they have been under.

Now they pass by the general, who sits a little behind General V—— D——, and near General Q——. Among the artillery, I saw the Lady Richardson, captured and brought away from Corinth. As they come on, and pass by General V—— D——, they salute; which is answered by his raising his cap to the colours, disclosing a proud, youthful head, surrounded by curls. He is immediately before me, and I do not see his face, which is marked with deep lines I have noticed before. In the evening, after the review, I attended a party given to the generals here collected. The house was crowded; the generals, with their staff and other officers, were there, and some of the lovely ladies of

Holly Springs. The supper was handsome. Toasts were drunk to Generals P—— and V—— D——, and all went merry, &c. But in the midst of a conversation, an officer told me that the Federal forces were advancing on Holly Springs, and that probably the Confederate forces would evacuate the town in a day or two. So, dear J—— there is no telling where I will be when I write next.

Jackson.

I know you are smiling, as you see Jackson written at the head of my letter—smiling to think hw systematically I have bowed myself out of one town after the other, as the Federal troops have bowed themselves in; yet you know the old saw, "*He that fights, and runs away*," &c.; though I can take no comfort in this, as fighting has been my abomination since the war began. I have always, in peaceful times, had an admiration for heroes in brilliant uniforms, and would now, if the hero could possibly assure me that the brilliant uniform would always be filled with life. But how can one feel a pleasure in the gilt trappings of a friend, when they know that they may possibly serve as an anxiously sought target for some sharpshooter. You do not wonder at my quotation in favor of a retrograde movement in this frame of mind, do you? For the last week or two I have passed from one state of excitement to another, so that I am glad indeed to find a quiet resting place.

From Holly Springs the army under Generals V—— D—— and P—— retreated to Abbeville, where they remained stationary for a time. One day the inhabitants of O—— were alarmed by the distant booming of cannon. A great excitement prevailed, and various rumours went the rounds. One that the Federal troops had reached the Tallahatchee; another that they had crossed, and a battle was progressing between the Federal and Confederate forces.

The town grew wide awake. Wagons passed and repassed. Numerous families were seen walking rapidly toward the depot, carriages filled with ladies and children driving swiftly in the same direction. My friends were preparing to leave also. I had received a telegram from M——, telling me to be in readiness to take my departure during the afternoon. My preparations were made. A gentleman came on the down train to accompany me, when, to our great disappointment, passengers were not allowed to go on the train, for the hospital patients were all to be taken off before passengers could be accommodated. My friend was, however, by particular favour, allowed to ride in a baggage car with my trunks.

The next day, Sunday, how little it seemed like the Sabbath! passenger trains were to run if the stores could all be transported. So a number of friends, with myself, took our seats quite early in the cars at the depot, and waited patiently hour after hour, hearing most distracting rumours, until my patience had become nearly exhausted.

In the afternoon, great was my joy on seeing M—— enter the car. The army was retreating from Abbeville. Our friends resolved to take their carriage and cross the country to Columbus. M—— said he could get an ambulance for me, but I would be obliged to keep up with the army, as the Federal forces were following closely. The cars were vacated quickly, and I saw the last of my friends. An ambulance came up, and I was soon riding rapidly southward. That night we stopped at a roadside house. During the next day the greater portion of the army passed by, and encamped below the house we were in for the night.

The next morning was gloomy, dark, and disagreeable. "While I waited for M—— to come with an ambulance, Gen. P—— invited me to ride with him. The roads were in the most miserable condition, and for a time we drove on a corduroy road.

Just imagine me, dear J——, on a corduroy road, jolting through a swamp, with my child in my arms; the general talking in the calmest and most urbane manner. Yet the gloom of the day was over me, and I felt dismally miserable. Soon the rain began to pour down. We were at this time on the high road, which became every moment worse, from the travel of the artillery, the greater portion of which was before us. Immediately behind the general's ambulance drove the carriage of a lady, who had been compelled, like myself, to abandon the cars.

How incessantly the rain poured down! Now and then the ambulance would drive on the side of the road, stopping to let the infantry pass. Poor fellows! wet and begrimed with mud, plodding with blankets and knapsacks strapped on their backs, and guns on their shoulders; troublesome accompaniments at any time—far more so now in the driving rain. At the foot of the hills we would frequently be obliged to halt, sometimes for an hour, awaiting the passage of the artillery over the brow of the ascent.

The Federal troops were close in the rear. The horses strained and pulled, but the mud was so deep and heavy that the wheels became clogged, and I looked anxiously up, expecting to see some huge cannon, impelled by its weight, return to the base of the hill. Frequently the soldiers would be obliged to wade through the deep ruts of mud on the hillside, and give a new impulse to some wavering piece, assisting the horses, and pushing the weighty gun-carriage with united strength.

In the rain sat the staff officers on their dripping horses; and, giving orders from the ambulance window, the old general urged on the men. I wondered at the patience, the kindness with which he spoke to all; rapidly and cheerily to the staff officers: "Ride on, and see what obstructs the road;" and in a tone of sympathy, through the rain, to the straggling soldier: "Keep up, men, keep up." "We camp near, do we?" he called out in clear tones to the inspector. And the men raised their drooping heads and pressed forward at the encouragement in the well-known voice. I see the power of kindness with these men, dear J——. There are few general officers in the Confederacy so well-beloved by their men as General P——, yet he is only kind and perfectly just.

That night we stopped beyond Water Valley, at a house where the poor hostess tried to make us comfortable, and gave us much of her company, telling us that she was "cousin to Stonewall Jackson's wife and Hill's wife;" but she "reckoned they did not know it, and wouldn't think much of it, if they did." She brought in a large baby, and sat down by the general's side, telling him that she was going to name that baby after him. The general was as affable as usual; but I frequently turned to the window to conceal my amusement.

Suddenly I was startled by her turning quickly to me, and asking if I "would ever think her any kin to Stonewall Jackson's wife and Hill's wife." Never having seen either of the above-named ladies, I conscientiously answered I did not know as I should.

Wakened by the bugle call the next morning, I hastily arose, and in a few moments was ready to depart. We had proceeded but five miles when an *aide-de-camp* rode up, and told General P—— that General Pemberton wished him to return to Water Valley immediately, as the Federal forces were quite near, and the Confederate soldiers must make a stand. We alighted and sat a few moments in a negro cabin. Then the general mounted and rode toward Water Valley, followed by his staff officers. The lady and myself proceeded on with the wagons beyond Coffeeville, where the train halted and prepared to camp for the night.

As yet I had not heard from M—— since he rode off with the general, and I scarcely knew what to do. The soldiers were thrown out on picket duty around the trains, as a Federal force was also to the left of us, near the little town of Charleston. Heavy skirmishing was going on at Water Valley, we were told. As no house was near, the gentleman who had charge of the lady and myself told us that he would put up a pleasant tent, and make us quite comfortable. So a tent was pitched on a little hillock near, and I rested comfortably during the night. Early in the morning we were on our way, the remainder of the army having come up. At length we reached Grenada in safety, yet sorely pressed by the Federal troops.

Thus you see, dear J——, that I am unlucky enough to be identified with some retreat or threatened city. From Memphis, or over the greater distance that separates us, we can span our love; and through all, I am

Yours.

A Soldier's Story of the

Siege of Vicksburg

Contents

Dedication

To the boys that fought the battles of the Civil War, this volume is dedicated. The pictures of their daily life in camp, on the march, and in battle, were drawn upon the field of action. May the memory of those deeds never perish, but ever remain fresh, as a part of the record of the historic times which knit us together as

COMRADES

Personal Reminiscence

May 1st, 1863.—Logan's Division, to which we belonged, embarked on transports, that had passed the batteries at Vicksburg and Grand Gulf, last night, about two miles below the latter place, where we had marched down the Louisiana levee to meet the boats. Crossing the Mississippi River, we landed at Bruinsburg, and left that place this forenoon at 10 o'clock, marching twelve miles over dusty roads and through a hilly and broken country. Although the boys were tired, their minds were diverted with the scenery of a new State. After crossing the great Mississippi, we bade farewell to Louisiana and its alligators, and are now inhaling the fragrance and delightful odours of Mississippi flowers. Arriving near Port Gibson about dark, found that the advance of McClernand's corps had defeated the enemy, who had marched out from Vicksburg to check our army.

The fight was quite spirited, and the rebels hotly and bravely contested every foot of ground, but they were overpowered, as they will be in every engagement they have with us. Having only two day's rations in our haversacks, guess we will have to eat rather sparingly of them, for our wagon train is not on the road. Should rations run short, we will have to forage off the country; but even the supplies from that source will not feed Grant's large army. We were well satisfied, however, that the stars and stripes were victorious, in this battle, without our assistance. We did not smell the battle afar off, but heard cannonading through the day, and fully expected to take a hand in it. When we stopped, as we supposed, for the night, our colonel drew the regiment into line, and said Gen. McPherson had asked him if his regiment was too wearied to follow the retreating enemy.

When the question was put to the men, everyone wanted to go, and started on the trail with the swiftness of fresh troops, marching as rapidly as possible until 10 o'clock, then camped in a ravine for the night. During this rapid movement, we did some skirmishing. The Confederate Army had retreated, and we made the tail of it fly over the road pretty lively.

The battle was fought, and the victory won;
Three cheers for the Union! The work was well done.

May 2nd.—As the sun peeped over the eastern horizon, we slipped out of camp and went our way rejoicing. Oh, how beautiful the morning; calm and pleasant, with the great variety of birds warbling, as though all was peace and quiet. When camping in the darkness of night, our surroundings astonish us in the broad day light. We scarcely know our next door neighbour until the morning light gleams upon him. While waiting orders to move, many thousand troops passed to the front, so I think our regiment will see another day pass with unbroken ranks. We have the very best fighting material in our regiment, and are ever ready for action, but are not particularly "spoiling for a fight." Our turn will come, as it did at Fort Donelson, Shiloh and many other fields of glory.

It is quite common to hear soldiers who have never seen the first fight say they are afraid they will never get any of the glories of this war. They never "spoil" for the second fight, but get glory enough in the first to last them. When our regiment was living upon soft bread and luxuries of sweet things from home, while camped in the rear of Covington, Kentucky, we thought that the war would be over and our names not be spread upon our banners as the victors in a battle. There is glory enough for all. We stopped awhile in Port Gibson, and the boys found a lot of blank bank currency of different denominations, upon the Port Gibson bank. They signed some of them, and it is quite common to see a private of yesterday a bank president today. This may not become a circulating medium to a very great extent, but it is not at all likely that it will be refused by the inhabitants along our route when tendered in payment for corn-bread, sweet potatoes, etc.

In the afternoon we stopped awhile, and taking advantage of the halt made coffee, which is generally done, whether it is noon or not. There is a wonderful stimulant in a cup of coffee, and as we require a great nerve tonic, coffee is eagerly sought after. Dick Hunt, of Company G, and Tom McVey, of Co. B, discovered a poor lonely confederate chicken by the roadside. By some hen strategem it had eluded the eyes of at least ten thousand Yankees, but when the 20th Ohio came along the searching eyes of these two members espied its place of con-

PORTER'S GUN-BOATS IN FRONT OF GRAND GULF.

cealment. They chased it under an outhouse, which was on stilts, as a great many of the southern houses are. Dick being rather the fleetest crawled under the house and secured the feathered prize, but Tom seeing his defeat in not securing a "preacher's dinner," found a coffee-pot under another corner of the house, which he brought to daylight, and it proved to be full of silver coin mostly dollars. These he traded off to the boys for paper, as he could not carry his load.

How foolish it is for the Southern people to flee and leave their beautiful property to the foe. We only want something to eat. There are some who would apply the torch to a deserted home, that would not do so if the owners remained in it. It is quite common here to build the chimneys on the outside of the houses, and I have noticed them still standing where the house had been burned. The march today, towards Black River, has been a very pleasant one. I suppose Grant knows where he is taking us to, for we don't, not having had any communications with him lately upon the subject.

May 3rd.—Called up early, and off on the march. Received a mail today, which was a welcome visitor to many, as it is the first one for some time. May they come oftener, and to every soldier. One poor fellow, who did not receive a letter, declared his girl had grown tired of him, and probably taken a beau at home. Another sympathized with him in the disappointment, and offered to let him read the letter he had received from his girl, who was aiding and encouraging him with her prayers. Pursued the enemy through the day, and were at their heels all the time, and at evening caught sight of them crossing Hankinson's Ferry, on Black River. We made a rapid charge upon them, firing as we ran, while DeGolier's battery shelled them. Some few were shot while crossing the bridge. I suppose they have retreated to Vicksburg, as they are on a direct road to that place. After driving the enemy across the temporary bridge, we closed up business for the night, and sought our blankets.

May 4th.—Early this morning the rebels planted a battery in the woods on the opposite side of the river, and sent shot and shell crashing into our camp. DeGolier's battery was soon in position, and silenced them before any damage was done. I hope DeGolier and his battery will be with us through all our engagements, for a braver man never lived. Some of his artillerymen said, he would rise up in his sleep, last night, and say, "give them canister, boys!"

I was detailed with a squad to patrol the river bank, and, in doing

120

Caisson.

Limber

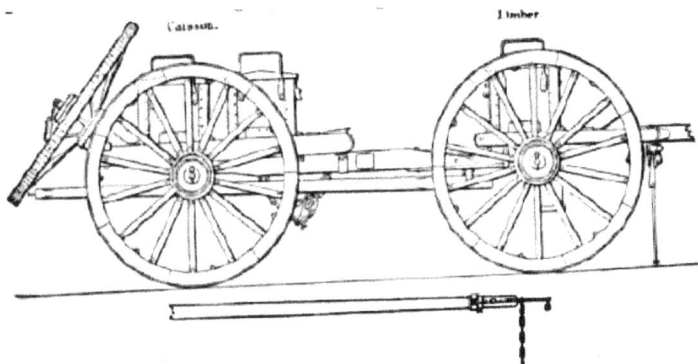

FIELD GUN-CARRIAGE.

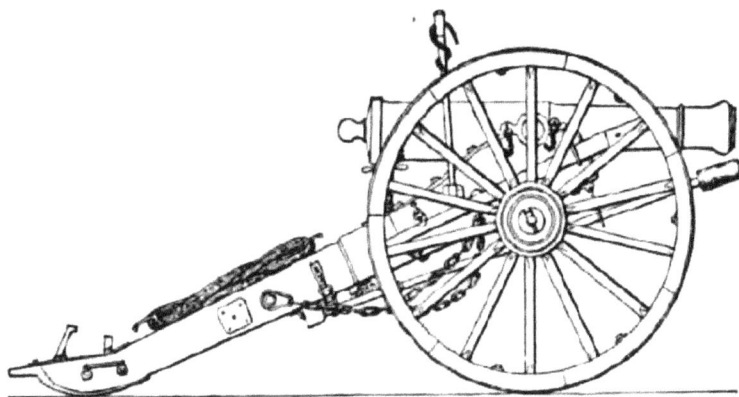

12-POUND HOWITZER

so, came in collision with the enemy. Some of the boys could not resist the temptation to take a swim. They did not think of the danger, until they were fired upon. When they went in, they complained of the water being cold; but they were not in long before it became too hot for them. They got out of that stream remarkably quick, and some did not stop to get their clothing, but flew for camp as naked as they were born. They did not know but the woods were full of rebels. A soldier's life has its share of fun as well as of the sad and marvellous.

I suppose this is considered an unsafe place to leave unguarded, so we remain another day.

May 5th.—We were annoyed some little through the night, by the rebels firing, but they didn't hit anybody. Two regiments of infantry with some cavalry crossed the river for a little scout. I do not think there are many rebels over there, but what few there are, ought to be whipped. They will have to fall back at the approach of our men, but that is easily done, and, when our forces return, they will be right back firing from behind the trees.

The army is marching on around Vicksburg, and we are very anxious to take our place in this grand column. We are quite tired of the duties assigned us here, and have had orders to move several times, which were as often countermanded.

Had chicken for dinner. Uncle Sam doesn't furnish chickens in his bill of fare, but they *will* get into the camp kettle. We have to be very saving of the regular rations, consequently must look outside for extras—chickens, ham, sweet potatoes, etc., all taste good. I walked down the river a short distance, viewing the scenery, when a bullet flew through the trees not far from my head. I looked across the river from whence it came, but could not see anybody. Did not stay there long, but got back to camp, where I felt safer.

Our camp is in the bottom, close to the river bank. The enemy at Grand Gulf spiked their cannon and retreated to Vicksburg. If that place could not be taken by the gun-boats on the river in front, the infantry marching in their rear made them hustle out in a hurry. When the people in Vicksburg see their retreating troops returning to the town, they went out to protect, they will think Grant's marching around them means something.

While writing a few letters today I was amused to notice the various attitudes taken by the boys while writing. One wrote on a drumhead, another on his cartridge-box; one used a board and several wrote on the top of a battery caisson. These letters would be more highly appreciated by the recipients if the circumstances under which they were prepared were realised.

May 6th.—This day has been a hot one, but as our duties have not been of an arduous nature we have sought the shade and kept quiet. While in camp, the boys very freely comment upon our destination, and give every detail of progress a general overhauling. The ranks of our volunteer regiments were filled at the first call for troops. That call opened the doors of both rich and poor, and out sprang merchant, farmer, lawyer, physician and mechanics of every calling, whose true and loyal hearts all beat in unison for their country. The first shot that struck Sumpter's wall sent an electric shot to every loyal breast, and today we have in our ranks material for future captains, colonels and generals, who before this war is ended will be sought out and honoured.

It cannot be possible that we are to be kept at this place much longer, for it is not very desirable as a permanent location. Of course we are here for some purpose, and I suppose that to be to prevent the enemy from assailing our line of supplies. As they are familiar with the country they can annoy us exceedingly without much loss to themselves. But after we have captured Vicksburg, and the history of Grant's movements is known, we shall then understand why we guarded Hankinson's Ferry so long. One of the boys said he thought Mr. Hankinson owed us something nice for taking such good care of his ferry for him. The variety of comments and opinions expressed in camp by the men is very curious. Some say we are going to surround Vicksburg, others think Grant is feeling for the enemy's weakest point there to strike him, and one cool head remarked that it was all right wherever we went while Grant was leading, for he had never known defeat.

Confidence in a good general stiffens a soldier—a rule that ought to work both ways. Surely no leader ever had more of the confidence of those he led than General Grant. He is not as social as McPherson, Sherman, Logan and some others, but seems all the while careful of the comfort of his men, with an eye single to success. Great responsibilities, perhaps, suppress his social qualities, for the present; for each day presents new obstacles to be met and overcome without delay. The enemy are doing all they can to hinder us, but let Grant say *forward*, and we obey.

Unable to sleep last night, I strolled about the camp awhile. Cause of my wakefulness, probably too much chicken yesterday. I appeared to be the only one in such a state, for the rest were

Lost in heavy slumbers.
Free from toil and strife,
Dreaming of their dear ones,
Home and child and wife;
Tentless they are lying.
While the moon shines bright.
Sleeping in their blankets.
Beneath the summer's night.

May 7th.—Our company detailed and reported this morning at headquarters for picket duty, but not being needed, returned to camp. Were somewhat disappointed, for we preferred a day on picket by way of change.

Pickets are the eyes of the army and the terror of those who live in close proximity to their line. Twenty-four hours on picket is hardly ever passed without some good foraging.

We broke camp at ten o'clock a. m., and very glad of it. After a pleasant tramp of ten miles we reached Rocky Springs. Here we have good, cold spring water, fresh from the bosom of the hills.

We have met several of the men of this section who have expressed surprise at the great number of troops passing. They think there must be a million of "you'ns" coming down here. We have assured them they have not seen half of our army. To our faces these citizens seem good Union men, but behind our backs, no doubt their sentiments undergo a change. Probably they were among those who fired at us, and will do it again as soon as they dare. I have not seen a regular acknowledged rebel since we crossed the river, except those we have seen in their army. They may well be surprised at the size of our force, for this. Vicksburg expedition is indeed a big thing, and I am afraid the people who were instrumental in plunging this country headlong into this war have not yet realised what evils they have waked up. They are just beginning to open their eyes to war's career of devastation.

They must not complain when they go out to the barnyard in the morning and find a hog or two missing at roll-call, or a few chickens less to pick corn and be picked in turn for the pot. I think these southern people will be benefited by the general diffusion of information which our army is introducing; and after the war new enterprise and better arts will follow—the steel plough, for instance, in place of the bull-tongue or old root that has been in use here so long to scratch the soil. The South must suffer, but out of that suffering will come wisdom.

May 8th.—We were ready to continue our march, but were not ordered out. Some white citizens came into camp to see the "Yankees," as they call us. Of course they do not know the meaning of the term, but apply it to all Union soldiers. They will think there are plenty of Yankees on this road if they watch it. The country here looks desolate. The owners of the plantations are "dun gone," and the fortunes of war have cleared away the fences. One of the boys foraged today and brought into camp, in his blanket, a variety of vegetables—and nothing is so palatable to us now as a vegetable meal, for we have been living a little too long on nothing but bacon. Pickles taste first-rate. I always write home for pickles, and I've a lady friend who makes and sends me, when she can, the best kind of "ketchup." There is nothing else I eat that makes me *catch up* so quick.

There is another article we learn to appreciate in camp, and that is newspapers—something fresh to read. The boys frequently bring in reading matter with their forage. Almost anything in print is better than nothing. A novel was brought in today, and as soon as it was caught sight of a score or more had engaged in turn the reading of it. It will soon be read to pieces, though handled as carefully as possible, under the circumstances. We cannot get reading supplies from home down here. I know papers have been sent to me, but I never got them. The health of our boys is good, and they are brimful of spirits (not "commissary"). We are generally better on the march than in camp, where we are too apt to get lazy, and grumble; but when moving we digest almost anything. When soldiers get bilious, they cannot be satisfied until they are set in motion.

May 9th.—Orders this morning to draw two days' rations, pack up and be ready to move at a moment's warning. We drew hard-tack, coffee, bacon, salt and sugar, and stored them in our haversacks. Some take great care so to pack the hard-tack that it will not dig into the side while marching, for if a corner sticks out too much anywhere, it is only too apt to leave its mark on the soldier. Bacon, too, must be so placed as not to grease the blouse or pants. I see many a bacon badge about me—generally in the region of the left hip. In filling canteens, if the covers get wet the moisture soaks through and scalds the skin.

The tin cup or coffee-can is generally tied to the canteen or else to the blanket or haversack, and it rattles along the road, reminding one of the sound of the old cow coming home.

All trifling troubles like these on the march may be easily forestalled by a little care, but care is something a soldier is not apt to take, and he too often packs his "grub" as hurriedly as he "bolts" it. We were soon ready to move, and filled our canteens with the best water we have had for months. We did not actually get our marching order, however, until near three o'clock p. m., so that being anxious to take fresh water with us, we had to empty and refill canteens several times. As we waited for the order, a good view was afforded us of the passing troops, and the bristling lines really looked as if there was war ahead.

Oh, what a grand army this is, and what a sight to fire the heart of a spectator with a speck of patriotism in his bosom. I shall never forget the scene of today, while looking back upon a mile of solid columns, m arching with their old tattered flags streaming in the summer breeze, and hearkening to the firm tramp of their broad brogans keeping step to the pealing fife and drum, or the regimental bands discoursing "*Yankee Doodle*" or "*The Girl I Left Behind Me.*" I say it was a grand spectacle—but how different the scene when we meet the foe advancing to the strains of "*Dixie*" and "*The Bonny Blue Flag.*"

True, I have no fears for the result of such a meeting, for we are marching full of the prestige of victory, while our foes have had little but defeat for the last two years. There is an inspiration in the memory of victory. Marching through this hostile country with large odds against us, we have crossed the great river and will cut our way through to Vicksburg, let what dangers may confront us. To turn back we should be overwhelmed with hosts exulting on their own native soil. These people can and will fight desperately, but they cannot put a barrier in our way that we cannot pass. Camped a little after dark.

May 10th.—Left camp after dinner. Dinner generally means noon, but our dinner-time on the march is quite irregular. Advanced unmolested till within about three miles of Utica, and camped again at dark.

This forenoon my bunk-mate (Cal. Waddle) and I went to a house near camp to get some corn-bread, but struck the wrong place, for we found the young mistress who had just been deserted by her negroes, all alone, crying, with but a scant allowance of provisions left her. She had never learned to cook, and in fact was a complete stranger to housework of any kind. Her time is now at hand to learn the great lesson of humanity. There has been a little too much idleness among these planters. But although I am glad the negroes are free I don't like to see them leaving a good home, for good homes some of them I know are leaving. They have caught the idea from some unknown source that freedom means fine dress, furniture, carriages and luxuries. Little do they yet know of the scripture—"*In the sweat of thy face shalt thou eat bread.*" I am for the Emancipation Proclamation, but I do not believe in cheating them.

This lady's husband is a confederate officer now in Vicksburg, who told her when he left she should never see a Yankee "down thar." Well, we had to tell her we were "thar," though, and to our question what she thought of us, after wiping her eyes her reply was we were very nice looking fellows. We were not fishing for compliments, but we like to get their opinions at sight, for they have been led, apparently, to expect to find the Lincoln soldier more of a beast than human. At least such is the belief among the lower sort. Negroes and poor whites here seem to be on an equality, so far as education is concerned and the respect of the better classes. I have not seen a single schoolhouse since I have been in Dixie, and I do not believe such a thing exists outside of their cities. But this war will revolutionise things, and among others I hope change this state of affairs for the better.

War is a keen analyser of a soldier's character. It reveals in camp, on the march and in battle the true principles of the man better than they are shown in the every-day walks of life. Here he has a chance to throw off the vicious habits of the past, and take such a stand as to gain a lasting reputation for good, or, if he dies upon the field, the glory of his achievements, noble 'deeds and soldierly bearing in camp will live in the memory of his comrades. Every soldier has a personal history to make, which will be agreeable, or not, as he chooses. A company of soldiers are as a family; and, if every member of it does his duty towards the promotion of good humour, much will be done toward softening the hardships of that sort of life.

This is Sunday, and few seem to realise it. I would not have known it myself but for my diary. I said, "boys this is Sunday." Somebody asked, "how do you know it is?" I replied my diary told me. Another remarked, "you ought to tell us then when Sunday comes round so we can try to be a little better than on week days." While in regular camps we have had preaching by the chaplains, but now that we are on the move that service is dispensed with, and what has become of the chaplains now I am unable to say. Probably buying and selling cotton, for some of them are regular tricksters, and think more of filling their own pockets with greenbacks than the hearts of soldiers with the word of God.

May 11th.—We drew two days' rations and marched till noon. My company, E, being detailed for rear guard, a very undesirable position. General Logan thinks we shall have a fight soon. I am not particularly anxious for one, but if it comes I will make my musket talk. As we contemplate a battle, those who have been spoiling for a fight cease to be heard. It does not even take the smell of powder to quiet their nerves—a rumour being quite sufficient.

We have no means of knowing the number of troops in Vicksburg, but if they were well generaled and thrown against us at some particular point, the matter might be decided without going any further. If they cannot whip us on our journey around their city, why do they not stay at home and strengthen their boasted position, and not lose so many men in battle to discourage the remainder? We are steadily advancing, and propose to keep on until we get them where they *can't* retreat. My fear is that they may cut our supply train, and then we should be in a bad fix. Should that happen and they get us real hungry, I am afraid short work would be made of taking Vicksburg.

Having seen the four great generals of this department, shall always feel honoured that I was a member of Force's 20th Ohio, Logan's Division, McPherson's Corps of Grant's Army. The expression upon the face of Grant was stern and care-worn, but determined. McPherson's was the most pleasant and courteous—a perfect gentleman and an officer that the 17th corps fairly worships. Sherman has a quicker and more dashing movement than some others, a long neck, rather sharp features, and altogether just such a man as might lead an army through the enemy's country. Logan is brave and does not seem to know what defeat means. We feel that he will bring us out of every fight victorious. I want no better or braver officers to fight under. I have often thought of the sacrifice that a general might make of his men in order to enhance his own *éclat*, for they do not always seem to display the good judgment they should. But I have no fear of a needless sacrifice of life through any mismanagement of this army.

May 12th.—Roused up early and before daylight marched, the 20th in the lead. Now we have the honoured position, and will probably get the first taste of battle. At nine o'clock slight skirmishing

THE RAID ON THE FENCE BEFORE GOING INTO CAMP

began in front, and at eleven we filed into a field on the right of the road, where another regiment joined us on our right, with two other regiments on the left of the road and a battery in the road itself. In this position our line marched down through open fields until we reached the fence, which we scaled and stacked arms in the edge of a piece of timber. No sooner had we done this than the boys fell to amusing themselves in various ways, taking little heed of the danger about to be entered. A group here and there were employed in *"euchre,"* for cards seem always handy enough where soldiers are. Another little squad was discussing the scenes of the morning. One soldier picked up several canteens, saying he would go ahead and see if he could fill then.

Soon after he disappeared, he returned with a quicker pace and with but one canteen full, saying, when asked why he came back so quick—"while I was filling the canteen I heard a noise, and looking up discovered several Johnnies behind trees, getting ready to shoot, and I concluded I would retire at once and report." Meanwhile my bedfellow had taken from his pocket a small mirror and was combing his hair and moustache. Said someone to him, "Cal., you needn't fix up so nice to go into battle, for the rebs won't think any better of you for it."

Just here the firing began in our front, and we got orders: "Attention! Fall in—take arms—forward—double-quick, march!" And we moved quite lively, as the rebel bullets did likewise. We had advanced but a short distance—probably a hundred yards—when we came to a creek, the bank of which was high, but down we slid, and wading through the water, which was up to our knees, dropped upon the opposite side and began firing at will. We did not have to be told to shoot, for the enemy were but a hundred yards in front of us, and it seemed to be in the minds of both officers and men that this was the very spot in which to settle the question of our right of way. They fought desperately, and no doubt they fully expected to whip us early in the fight, before we could get reinforcements.

There was no bank in front to protect my company, and the space between us and the foe was open and perfectly level. Every man of us knew it would be sure death to all to retreat, for we had behind us a bank seven feet high, made slippery by the wading and climbing back of the wounded, and where the foe could be at our heels in a moment. However, we had no idea of retreating, had the ground been twice as inviting; but taking in the situation only strung us up to higher de-

DeGolier's Battery going Into action at the
Battle of Raymond.

John Calvin Waddell,
Corporal Co. E, 20th Ohio,
killed May 12 1863

termination. The regiment to the right of us was giving way, but just as the line was wavering and about to be hopelessly broken, Logan dashed up, and with the shriek of an eagle tamed them back to their places, which they regained and held. Had it not been for Logan's timely intervention, who was continually riding up and down the line, firing the men with his own enthusiasm, our line would undoubtedly have been broken at some point.

For two hours the contest raged furiously, but as man after man dropped dead or wounded, the rest were inspired the more firmly to hold fast their places and avenge the fallen. The creek was running red with precious blood spilt for our country. My bunk-mate and I were kneeling side by side when a ball crashed through his brain, and he fell over with a mortal wound. With the assistance of two others I picked him up, carried him over the bank in our rear, and laid behind a tree, removing from his pocket, watch and trinkets, and the same little mirror that had helped him make his last toilet but a little while before. We then went back to our company after an absence of but a few minutes. Shot and shell from the enemy came over thicker and faster, while the trees rained bunches of twigs around us.

One by one the boys were dropping out of my company. The second lieutenant in command was wounded; the orderly sergeant dropped dead, and I find myself (fifth sergeant) in command of the handful remaining. In front of us was a reb in a red shirt, when one of our boys, raising his gun, remarked, "see me bring that red shirt down," while another cried out, "hold on, that is my man." Both fired, and the red shirt fell—it may be riddled by more than those two shots. A red shirt is, of course, rather too conspicuous on a battlefield. Into another part of the line the enemy chained, fighting hand to hand, being too close to fire, and using the butts of their guns. But they were all forced to give way at last, and we followed them up for a short distance, when we were passed by our own reinforcements coming up just as we had whipped the enemy.

I took the roll-book from the pocket of our dead sergeant, and found that while we had gone in with thirty-two men, we came out with but sixteen—one-half of the brave little band, but a few hours before be full of hope and patriotism, either killed or wounded. Nearly all the survivors could show bullet marks in clothing or flesh, but no man left the field on account of wounds. When I told Colonel Force of our loss, I saw tears course down his cheeks, and so intent were his thoughts upon his fallen men that he failed to note the bursting of a shell above him, scattering the powder over his person, as he sat at the foot of a tree.

Although our ranks have been so thinned by today's battle our will is stronger than ever to march and fight on, and avenge the death of those we must leave behind. I am very sad on account of the loss of so many of my comrades, especially the one who bunked with me, and who had been to me like a brother, even sharing my load when it grew burdensome. He has fallen; may he sleep quietly under the shadows of those old oaks which looked down upon the struggle of today.

We moved up to the town of Raymond and there camped. I suppose this will be named the Battle of Raymond. The citizens had prepared a good dinner for the rebels on their return from victory, but as they actually returned from defeat they were in too much of a hurry to enjoy it. It is amusing now to hear the boys relating their experiences going into battle. All agree that to be under fire without the privilege of returning it is uncomfortable—a feeling which soon wears off when their own firing begins. I suppose the sensations of our boys are as varied as their individualities. No matter how brave a man may be, when he first faces the muskets and cannon of an enemy he is seized with a certain degree of fear, and to some it becomes an occasion of an involuntary but very sober review of their past lives. There is now little time for meditation; scenes change rapidly; he quickly resolves to do better if spared, but when afterward marching from a victorious field such good resolutions are easily forgotten. I confess, with humble pleasure, that I have never neglected to ask God's protection when going into a fight, nor thanking him for the privilege of coming out again alive. The only thought that troubles me is that of falling into an unknown grave.

The battle today opened very suddenly, and when DeGolier's battery began to thunder, while the infantry fire was like the pattering of a shower, some cooks, happening to be surprised near the front, broke for the rear carrying their utensils. One of them with a kettle in his hand, rushing at the top of his speed, met General Logan, who halted him, asking where he was going, when the cook piteously cried, "Oh General, I've got no gun, and such a snapping and cracking as there is up yonder I never heard before." The general let him pass to the rear.

Thomas Runyan,[1] of Company A, was wounded by a musket ball

---

1. Note.—When the regiment was being mustered out in July, 1865, Thomas Runyan. who had been left for dead, visited the regiment. He said he came "to see the boys." He was, of course, totally blind.

HAND-TO-HAND COMBAT

THE RAIN CAME DOWN IN PERFECT TORRENTS.

which entered the right eye, and passing behind the left forced it out upon his cheek. As the regiment passed, I saw him lying by the side of the road, tearing the ground in his death struggle.

May 13th.—Up early, and on the march to Jackson, as we suppose.

I dreamed of my bunk-mate last night. Wonder if his remains will be put where they can be found, for I would like, if I ever get the chance, to put a board with his name on it at the head of his grave. When we enlisted we all paired off, each selecting his comrade—such a one as would be congenial and agreeable to him—and as yesterday's battle broke a good many such bonds, new ties have been forming,— as the boys say, new couples are getting married. If married people could always live as congenial and content as two soldiers sleeping under the same blanket, there would be more happiness in the world. I shall await the return of one of the wounded.

We arrived at Clinton after dark, a place on the Jackson and Vicksburg railroad. Yesterday a train ran through, the last that will ever be run by confederates. The orders are to destroy the road here in each direction. We expected to have to fight for this spot, but instead we took possession unmolested. "Cotton is king," and finding a good deal here, we have made our beds of it.

May 14th.—Started again this morning for Jackson. When within five miles of the city we heard heavy firing. It has rained hard today and we have had both a wet and muddy time, pushing at the heavy artillery and provision wagons accompanying us when they stuck in the mud. The rain came down in perfect torrents. What a sight! Ambulances creeping along at the side of the track—artillery toiling in the deep ruts while generals with their aids and orderlies splashed mud and water in every direction in passing. We were all wet to the skin, but plodded on patiently, for the love of country.

When within a few miles of Jackson, the news reached us that Sherman had slipped round to the right and captured the place, and the shout that went up from the men on the receipt of that news was invigorating to them in the midst of trouble. I think they could have been heard in Jackson. Sherman's army at the right and McPherson in our immediate front, with one desperate charge we ran without stopping till we reached the town. The flower of the confederate forces, the pride of the Southern States who had never yet known defeat, came up to Jackson last night to help demolish Grant's army, but for once they failed. Veterans of Georgia stationed as reserves were also forced to yield in dismay, and never stopped retreating till they had passed far south of the Capital which they had striven so valiantly to defend. Tonight the stars and stripes float proudly over the cupola of the seat of government of Mississippi—and if my own regiment has not had a chance today to cover itself with glory it has with mud.

I shall not soon forget the conversation I have had with a wounded rebel. He said that his regiment last night was full of men who had never before met us, and who felt sure it would be easy to whip us. How they were deceived! He said part of his regiment was behind a hedge fence, where they felt comparatively safe, but the Yankees jumped right over without stopping, and swept everything before them. I never saw finer looking men than the killed and wounded rebels of today, and with the smooth face of one of them, lying in a garden mortally wounded, I was so taken, that I eased his thirst with a drink from my own canteen. His piteous glance at me at that time I shall never forget.

It is on the battlefield and among the dead and dying we get to know each other better—nay, even our own selves. Administering to a stranger, we think of his mother's love, as dear to him as our own to us. When the fight is over, away all bitterness. Let us leave with the foe some tokens of good will, that, when the cruel war at last is over, may be kindly remembered. I trust our enemies may yet be led to hail in good faith the return of peace and the restoration of the Union. This is a domestic war, the saddest of all, being fought between those whose hearts should be as brothers; and when it is at an end, may those hearts again throb together beneath the folds of the flag that once waved for defence over their sires and themselves—a flag whose proud motto will be, *"peace on earth and good will to men."*

Some of the boys went down into the city to view our new possession. It seems ablaze, but I trust only public property is being destroyed, or such as might aid and comfort the enemy hereafter.

I am very tired, and of course can easily get excused, so I will go to my bed on the ground.

May 15th.—The familiar "Attention, battalion!" was heard from our colonel, when we marched back upon the same road that had led us to Jackson, camping as usual at dark. We passed through Clinton, and the inhabitants were surprised to see us returning so soon, for they fully expected to hear of our being defeated and driven back.

But they did not know our metal. The last few days have been full of excitement, and although we have marched and fought hard, and lost some of our best men, besides getting tired and hungry ourselves, we are more resolved than ever to keep the ball rolling. The thinner our ranks are made by fighting and disease, the closer together the remnants are brought. We shall close up the ranks and press forward until the foe is vanquished. Soldiers grow more friendly as they are brought better to realise the terrible ravages of war.

As Colonel Force called us to "Attention!" this morning, one of the boys remarked, "I love that man more than ever." Yes, we have good reason to be proud of our colonel, for upon all occasions we are treated by him as volunteers enlisted in war from pure love of country, and not regulars, drawn into service from various other motives, in time of peace.

May 16th.—We rolled out of bed this morning early, and had our breakfast of slapjacks made of flour, salt and water, which lie on a man's stomach like cakes of lead—for we are out of all rations but flour and salt, though we hope soon for some variety. We heard heavy firing about eleven o'clock. Our division reached Champion Hill about two p. m., and filed into a field on the right of the road. We were drawn up in a line facing the woods through which ran the road we had just left. It was by this road the rebels came out of Vicksburg to whip us. We had orders to lie down. The command was obeyed with alacrity, for bullets were already whizzing over our heads. I never hugged Dixie's soil as close as I have today. We crowded together as tight as we could, fairly ploughing our faces into the ground. Occasionally a ball would pick its man in spite of precaution, and he would have to slip to the rear. Soon we got orders to rise up, and in an instant every man was on his feet. If the former order was well obeyed, the latter was equally so.

The enemy charged out of the woods in front of us in a solid line, and as they were climbing the fence between us, which separated the open field from the timber, DeGolier's battery, stationed in our front, opened on them with grape and canister, and completely annihilated men and fence, and forced the enemy to fall back. Such terrible execution by a battery I never saw. It seemed as if every shell burst just as it reached the fence, and rails and rebs flew into the air together. They, finding our centre too strong, renewed their charge on our left, and succeeded in driving it a short distance, but their success was only for a moment, for our boys rallied, and with reinforcements drove them in turn. We now charged into the woods and drove them a little ways, and as we charged over the spot so lately occupied by the foe, we saw the destruction caused by our battery, the ground being covered thickly with rebel grey. When we reached the woods we were exposed to a galling fire, and were at one time nearly surrounded, but we fought there hard until our ammunition was exhausted, when we fixed bayonets and prepared to hold our ground. A fresh supply of ammunition soon came up, when we felt all was well with us again. Meanwhile the right of our line succeeded in getting around to their left, when the enemy retreated towards Vicksburg, lest they should be cut off.

The battle today was commenced early in the morning by Mc-Clernand's great fighting corps, and was a hot and severe contest, until Logan's division approached the road on the Confederates' left, between them and Vicksburg, when the foe wavered and began to break. This was a hard day's fight, for the rebels, finding that they had been beaten in three battles about Vicksburg, had no doubt resolved to make a desperate stand against our conquering march; but alas! for them, this day's course of events was like the rest. When the fight was over. Generals Grant, McClernand, Sherman, McPherson and Logan rode over the victorious field, greeted with the wildest cheers. I wonder if they love their men as we love them. We received our mail an hour or two after the fight, and the fierce struggle through which we had just passed was forgotten as we read the news from home. Our fingers fresh from the field left powder marks on the white messengers that had come to cheer us.

Our forces captured eleven pieces of artillery and over one thousand prisoners. The retreating army will make another stand, but we shall move right on, undaunted. Several amusing incidents have occurred during the battle today. Company A, of the 20th, was sent out to skirmish, and moved forward till they could see the enemy. By this time General Logan made his appearance, when one of the boys who wished to go into the fight without impediments, approached Logan and said, "General, shall we not unsling knapsacks?"

"No," was the stern reply, "damn them, you can whip them with your knapsacks on."

This same company, in full view of a rebel battery, had taken refuge in a deep ditch, and when afterward the rebel captain cried out, "ready, take aim," Mit. Bryant, feeling secure in his position, interrupted the

CROCKER, HOVEY AND LOGAN'S DIVISIONS DRIVING THE ENEMY AT THE POINT OF THE BAYONET THROUGH CHAMPION HILLS

order with a shout, "shoot away and be damned to you."

We moved up through the woods to the road again after the fight, where we halted an hour. Near the road was a farm house which was immediately taken possession of for a hospital.

May 17th.—On the road to Vicksburg, resolved to capture the city or get badly whipped. We have not known defeat since we left Fort Donelson, and we propose to keep our good record up. We have seen hard times on some hotly contested fields, but mean to have nothing but victory, if possible, on our banner.

The advance of our army has made a grand sweep, pell-mell, over the rebel works at Big Black River, routing the foe and capturing twenty-five hundred prisoners with twenty-nine cannon. Their rifle pits were quite numerous, but they were all on low ground, so that when the word was given the Yankees rushed over them with the greatest ease. The rebs may be drawing us into a trap, but as yet we have not a moments' fear of the result, for when Grant tells us to go over a thing we go, and feel safe in going. Even in time of peace we would not wish the great curtain that hides the future to be rolled away, nor do soldiers now ask to know what lies before them. But every day brings new scenes fraught with dangers, hair-breadth escapes or death, after which the ranks close and move on undaunted. And our love of country still grows as we go.

We camped within a few miles of Black River, perfectly satisfied, though we have had no hand in the slaughter today. We rather expected to be halted a few days at the river, where the enemy would surely be strongly fortified, and where, as they could certainly spare the greater part of their forces from Vicksburg, if they would but bring them out, they could make a desperate stand. We are now fighting hard for our *grub*, since we have nothing left but flour and slapjacks lie too heavy on a soldier's stomach. But there is great consolation in reflecting that behind us Uncle Sam keeps piled a bountiful supply all ready to be issued as soon as we can find a proper halting place.

May 18th.—The army last night made pontoons, on which this morning the Black River has been crossed. McClernand is on the left, McPherson in the centre, and Sherman on the right. In this position the three great corps will move to Vicksburg by different roads. We are nearing the doomed city, and are now on the lookout for fun.

As we crossed the river and marched up the bank, a brass band stood playing national airs. Oh, how proud we felt as we marched

Breakfast,	-	Slapjacks.
Dinner,	- -	Slapjacks.
Supper,	-	Slapjacks.

TOO MANY SLAPJACKS CAUSE A SOLDIER TO DREAM
OF A FEAST AT HOME.

SHERMAN'S MEN INFLATING RUBBER PONTOON ON WHICH TO
CROSS BIG BLACK RIVER

through the rebel works, and up to the muzzles of the abandoned guns that had been planted to stay our progress. Every man felt the combined Confederate Army could not keep us out of Vicksburg. It was a grand sight, the long lines of infantry moving over the pontoons, and winding their way up the bluffs, with flags flying in the breeze, and the morning sun glancing upon the guns as they lay across the shoulders of the boys. Cheer after cheer went up in welcome and triumph from the thousands who had already crossed and stood in waiting lines upon the bluff above. This is supposed to be the last halting place before we knock for admittance at our goal—the boasted Gibraltar of the west.

Our division has made a long march today, and we have bivouacked for the night without supper, and with no prospect of breakfast, for our rations have been entirely exhausted. Murmurings and complaints are loud and deep, and the swearing fully up to the army standard. General Leggett walked into our camp, and in his usual happy way inquired, "Well, boys, have you had your supper?"

"No, General, we have not had any."

"Well, boys, I have not had any either, and we shall probably have to fight for our breakfast."

"Very well. General; guess we can stand it as well as you," came the ready answer from a score of us, and resignation settled back upon the features of tired and hungry, but unsubdued, patriot soldiers.

You may study the hopeful, bright brows of these men.
Who have marched all day over hill and through glen,
Half clad and unfed; but who is it will dare
Claim to find on those faces one trace of despair?

May 19th.—This day beholds a cordon of steel, with rivets of brave hearts, surrounding Vicksburg. The enemy left their fortifications on the first, twelfth, fourteenth, sixteenth and eighteenth of this month, and dealt their best blows to prevent the occurrence of what we have just accomplished—the surrounding of their well fortified city. We have now come here to compel them to surrender, and we are prepared to do it either by charge or by siege, and they cannot say to us nay. They have fought well to keep their homes free from invasion, and surely deserve praise for their brave return to battle after so many defeats. Our army encircles the city from the river above to the river below, a distance of seven and a half miles.

The three corps have taken respective positions as follows: Sherman's Fifteenth occupies the right of the line, resting on the river above; General McClernand's Thirteenth touches the river below, while McPherson's Seventeenth stands in the centre. Our own division, commanded by Logan, occupies the road leading to Jackson.

In taking our position we did a great deal of skirmishing, and I suppose the same difficulty was probably experienced by the rest of the line. We have been nineteen days on the march around Vicksburg, and the time has been full of excitement—quite too varied for a comprehensive view just now, but those who have borne a part in it will store it all away in memory, to be gone over between comrades by piece-meal, when they meet after the war is over.

The personal experience of even the humblest soldier will get a hearing in years to come, for it is the little things in an unusual life that are most entertaining, and personal observations from the rank and file, narrated by those who saw what they describe, will make some of the most instructive paragraphs of the war's history.

This has been a day to try the nerves of the boys, while taking position in front to invest the doomed city. It has been a day to try men's souls, and hearts, too. The long lines of rebel earthworks following the zigzag courses of the hills, and black field guns still menacing from their port-holes, bristle with defiance to the invaders.

Our regiment, the 20th Ohio, being ordered in position on the Jackson road, immediately passed to the left in front of Fort Hill, where it stood ready to charge at a moment's notice. Meanwhile Colonel Force cautiously made his way in front of the different companies and spoke familiarly to his men words of encouragement. Said he, "boys, I expect we shall be ordered to charge the fort. I shall run right at it, and I hope every man will follow me." At that instant a soldier of one of the companies on the left was found snugly hid in a ravine under the roots of a tree, and his lieutenant's attention being called to the fact, he was ordered out, when he replied, "Lieutenant, I do not believe I am able to make such a charge."

May 20th.—When I awoke this morning I offered thanks to God that my life had been spared thus far. We slept on our arms—something unusual. This day has been busily spent in making cautious advances toward the works of the enemy, and, although our progress seems to have been very little, we are content to approach step by step, for the task is difficult and dangerous. Bullets are flying over our heads, and it is quite common to see the boys trying to dodge them.

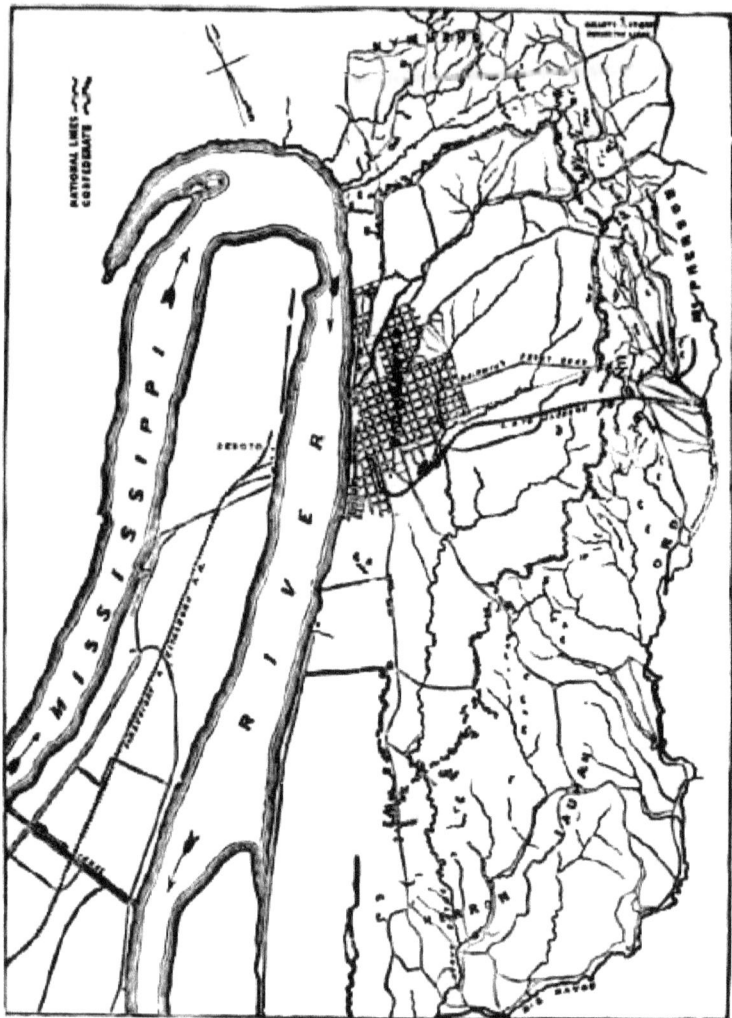

Map of Vicksburg, showing the river front and the positions of the Union and Confederate lines in the rear

A few have succeeded in stopping these bullets, but they had to leave at once for the hospital. A blanket displayed by its owner was called a map of the confederacy, on account of the holes in it made by bullets at Raymond and Champion Hills. It is good enough yet for warmth, but will not do to hold water. We are ragged and dirty, for we have had no change of clothes for over a month. But we have the promise of new suits soon. If we were to enter Vicksburg to-morrow, some of our nice young fellows would feel ashamed to march before the young ladies there. We can see the court house in the city with a confederate flag floating over it. What fun it will be to take that down, and hoist in its stead the old stars and stripes.

Then yonder is the Mississippi River again; we want to jump into that once more and have a good bath. The hills back of Vicksburg, and in fact all round the city seem quite steep and barren, and to run in parallels, affording our troops good shelter from batteries and secret approaches. It is upon these hills opposite the town that our tents are pitched. We must cut back into the hills to escape the shower of bullets, for we like to feel secure, when asleep or off duty. A great many of the balls that come over are what are called "spent," that is, have not force enough left to do any harm. We do not feel quite as safe awake or asleep as we did before we got so near the city. However, we manage to sleep pretty much unconcerned as to danger. Our regiment is detailed to watch at the rifle pits in front tonight.

May 21st.—We were relieved this morning before daylight, and slipped back to our camp as quietly as we could. The rifle pits where we watched were pretty close to the enemy, and we had to note every movement made by them. If they put their heads above their works we sent a hundred or more shots at them, and on the other hand, if any on our side made themselves too conspicuous, they fired in turn. So each army is watching the other like eagles. We must be relieved while it is yet dark, for if such a move were attempted by daylight, the enemy could get our range and drop many a man.

The weather is getting very hot, but we do our best to keep cool whether out of battle or in it. It is fortunate for us that our work at the rifle pits occurs at night, when the air is much more cool and pleasant, and the services less fraught with danger. Last night quite a number of new pits were opened and gabions placed on them. Firing from behind these was attended with less danger. Gabions are a sort of wicker-work, resembling round baskets, filled with dirt. The rebel fort in our front was made by cutting away the back half of the hill, leaving the face towards us in a state of nature. This fort is supplied with large guns, but their owners cannot use them, as our rifle pits occupy higher ground, from which we watch them too closely.

May 22nd.—Last night mortar-shells, fired from the boats on the river in front of the city across Point Louisiana, fell thick over all parts of Vicksburg, and at three o'clock this morning every cannon along our line belched its shot at the enemy. Nothing could be heard at the time but the thundering of great guns—one hundred cannons sent crashing into the town—parrot, shrapnel, canister, grape and solid shot—until it seemed impossible that anything could withstand such a fearful hailstorm. It was indeed a terrible spectacle—awfully grand.

At ten o'clock we had orders to advance. The boys were expecting the order and were busy divesting themselves of watches, rings, pictures and other keepsakes, which were being placed in the custody of the cooks, who were not expected to go into action. I never saw such a scene before, nor do I ever want to see it again. The instructions left with the keepsakes were varied. For instance, "This watch I want you to send to my father if I never return"—"I am going to Vicksburg, and if I do not get back just send these little trifles home, will you?"—proper addresses for the sending of the articles being left with them. Not a bit of sadness or fear appears in the talk or faces of the boys, but they thought it timely and proper to dispose of what they had accordingly.

This was done while we awaited orders, which at last came in earnest, and in obedience to them we moved up and took our place in the rifle pits within a hundred yards of Fort Hill, where we had orders to keep a diligent watch, and to fire at the first head that dared to show itself. The air was so thick with the smoke of cannon that we could hardly see a hundred yards before us. The line to our right and left was completely hidden from view except as revealed by the flash of guns, and the occasional bursting of shells through the dense clouds. About eleven o'clock came a signal for the entire line to charge upon the works of the enemy. Our boys were all ready, and in an instant leaped forward to find victory or defeat.

The Seventh Missouri took the lead with ladders which they placed against the fort, and then gave way for others to scale them. Those who climbed to the top of the fort met cold steel, and, when at length it was found impossible to enter the fort that way, the com-

146

mand was given to fall back, which was done under a perfect hail of lead from the enemy. The rebels, in their excitement and haste to fire at our retreating force, thrust their heads a little too high above their cover,—an advantage we were quick to seize with well aimed volleys. In this charge a severe loss was met by our division, and nothing gained. What success was met by the rest of the line I cannot say, but I hope it was better than ours. Thus ended another day of bloody fight in vain, except for an increase of the knowledge which has been steadily growing lately, that a regular siege will be required to take Vicksburg. This day will be eventful on the page of history, for its duties have been severe, and many a brave patriot bit the dust under the storm of deadly fire that assailed us.

May 23rd.—Our regiment lay in the rifle pits today, watching the enemy. For hours we were unable to see the motion of a man or beast on their side, all was so exceedingly quiet throughout the day. After dark we were relieved and as we returned to the camp the enemy got range of us, and for a few minutes their bullets flew about us quite freely However we bent our heads as low as we could and doublequicked to quarters. One shot flew very close to my head, and I could distinctly recognize the familiar zip and whiz of quite a number of others at a safer distance. The rebels seemed to fire without any definite direction. If our sharpshooters were not on the alert, the rebels could peep over their works and take good aim; but as they were m closely watched they had to be content with random shooting.

If this siege is to last a month there will be a whole army of trained sharpshooters, for the practice we are getting is making us skilled marksmen. I have gathered quite a collection of balls, which I mean to send home as relics of the siege. They are in a variety of shapes, and were a thousand brought together there could not be found two alike. I have picked up some that fell at my feet—others were taken from trees. I am the only known collector of such souvenirs, and have many odd and rare specimens. Rebel bullets are very common about here now—too much so to be valuable; and as a general thing the boys are quite willing to let them lie where they drop. I think, however, should I survive, I would like to look at them again in after years.

Shovel and pick are more in use today, which seems to be a sign that digging is to take the place of charging at the enemy. We think Grant's head is level, anyhow. The weather is getting hotter, and I fear sickness; and water is growing scarce, which is very annoying. If we

MORTAR FROM THE RIVER IN FRONT. "*DURING THE SIEGE OF VICKSBURG, SIXTEEN THOUSAND SHELLS WERE THROWN FROM THE MORTAR GUN-BOATS, AND NAVAL BATTERIES INTO THE CITY.*"—HAMERSLY.

BURYING THE DEAD THAT HAD LAIN BETWEEN THE UNION AND CONFEDERATE LINES FOR THREE DAYS.

can but keep well, the future has no fears for us.

May 24th.—Sunday; and how little like the Sabbath day it seems. Cannon are still sending their messengers of death into the enemy's lines, as on week days, and the minnie balls sing the same song, while the shovel throws up as much dirt as on any other day. What a relief it would be if, by common consent, both armies should cease firing today. It is our regiment's turn to watch at the front, so before daylight we moved up and took our position. We placed our muskets across the rifle pits, pointing towards the fort, and then lay down and ran our eyes over the gun, with finger on trigger, ready to fire at anything we might see moving. For hours not a movement was seen, till finally an old half-starved mule meandered too close to our lines, when off went a hundred or more muskets, and down fell the poor mule. This little incident, for a few minutes, broke the monotony.

A coat and hat were elevated on a stick above our rifle pits, and in an instant they were riddled with bullets from the enemy. The rebels were a little excited at the ruse, and probably thought, after their firing, there must be one less Yankee in our camp. In their eagerness a few of them raised their heads a little above their breastworks, when a hundred bullets flew at them from our side. They all dropped instantly, and we could not tell whether they were hit or not. The rebels, as well as ourselves, occasionally hold up a hat by way of diversion. A shell from an enemy's gun dropped into our camp rather unexpectedly, and bursted near a group, wounding several, but only slightly, though the doctor thinks one of the wounded will not be able to sit down comfortably for a few days. I suppose, then, he can go on picket, or walk around and enjoy the country.

May 25th.—Pemberton sent a flag of truce to Grant at two p. m., and the cessation of hostilities thus agreed on, lasted till eight o'clock in the evening. It made us happy, for we fancied it was a sign they wanted to surrender—but no such good luck. It was simply to give both sides a chance to bury their dead, which had been lying exposed since the twenty-second. Both armies issued from their respective fortifications and pits, and mingled together in various sports, apparently with much enjoyment. Here a group of four played cards—two Yanks and two Rebs. There, others were jumping, while everywhere blue and gray mingled in conversation over the scenes which had transpired since our visit to the neighbourhood.

I talked with a very sensible rebel who said he was satisfied we

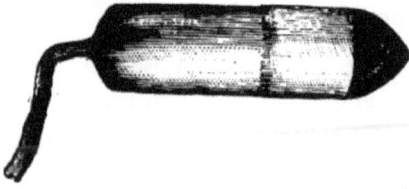

How swift their flight;
  What strange wierd music do they make;
And then, at last,
  What curious forms these little minnies take.

MINNIE BALLS FIRED AT VICKSBURG

RIFLE-MUSKET AND APPENDAGES

Vice,   Punch,   Ball-   Screw-   Wiper.
                     screw,   driver,

should not only take Vicksburg but drive the forces of the south all over their territory, at last compelling them to surrender; still, he said, he had gone into the fight, and was resolved not to back out. He said they had great hope of dissension in the north, to such an extent as might strengthen their cause. There have been grounds for this hope, I am sorry to say, and such dissensions at the north must prolong the war, if our peace party should succeed in materially obstructing the war measures of government. From the remarks of some of the rebels, I judged that their supply of provisions was getting low, and that they had no source from which to draw more. We gave them from our own rations some fat meat, crackers, coffee and so forth, in order to make, them as happy as we could. We could see plainly that their officers watched our communications closely.

May 26th.—Up this morning at three o'clock, with orders for three days' rations in our haversacks and five days' in the wagons—also to be ready to move at ten o'clock to the rear, in pursuit of Johnston, who was thrusting his bayonets too close to our boys there.

I am not anxious to get away from the front, yet a little marching in the country will be quite a desirable change, and no doubt beneficial to our men. I have been afraid we might be molested in the rear, for we were having our own way too smoothly to last. I think the confederate authorities are making a great mistake in not massing a powerful army in our rear and thus attempting to break our lines and raise the siege. We shall attend to Johnston, for Grant has planted his line so firmly that he can spare half his men to look out for his rear. What a change we notice today, from the time spent around the city, where there was no sound except from the zipping bullets and booming cannon; while out here in the country the birds sing as sweetly as if they had not heard of war at all. Here, too, we get an exchange from the smoky atmosphere around Vicksburg, to heaven's purest breezes.

We have marched today over the same ground for which we fought to gain our position near the city. Under these large spreading oaks rest the noble dead who fell so lately for their country. This march has been a surprise to me. It is midnight, and we are still marching.

May 27th.—It was three o'clock this morning before we camped. A tiresome tramp we have had, and after halting, but a few minutes elapsed before we were fast asleep. We were up, however, with the sun, took breakfast and were on the march again at eight o'clock. We halted two hours at noon, during which time we had dinner and rest.

Camped again in the evening without having come in contact with the enemy. We do not know where Johnston is, but shall find him if he is in the neighbourhood. This excursion party is composed of six regiments, and should we meet Johnston, and his force prove to be the largest, we shall have to fight hard, for we are now some distance from reinforcements. The health of our boys, however, is good—although one of them complains of *worms*—in his crackers. A change from city to country life seems generally acceptable—and yet as it was, our residence was only suburban.

May 28th.—We did not strike out on the war-path again till three p. m. today, having spent the time previous in taking a good rest. Today we have not marched very rapidly, as it has now become necessary to go more slowly in order to feel our way, since we cannot tell what obstacle we may encounter. All the natives we meet along the road claim that Johnston is going to raise the siege. If so, it will prove about the biggest "raising" he ever attended. Camped again about dark.

May 29th.—"*The early bird catches the worm.*" We tried the truth of that adage this morning, but failed to make the catch. A few graybacks were seen afar off, but we failed to get within range of them. Where, where, is General Johnston and the grand army he was to bring against us? We have looked for him in vain. I have the utmost confidence in Grant's judgment and the prestige of his army which has never yet known defeat, but I confess, till now, I have been afraid of some attack in our rear. And why such a thing does not occur is a mystery to me—at least an attempt at it. Day by day Grant is intrenching and pushing nearer to the enemy's works, planting heavy guns and receiving fresh troops, so the opportunity for a saving stroke by the enemy is fast disappearing.

Camped again at dark, within two miles of Mechanicsville, through which we passed, finding all quiet after our cavalry had driven a few rebs beyond the town.

May 30th.—Moved this morning at four o'clock back again towards Vicksburg—rather an early start, unless some special business awaits us. A few surmise that there is need for us at the front, but I think it is only a freak of General Frank Blair, who is in command of our excursion party. The day has been hot, and we have been rushed forward as though the salvation of the Union depended upon our forced march. I am not a constitutional grumbler, but I fail to understand why we have been trotted through this sultry Yazoo bottom where pure air seems to be a stranger. Probably our commander wants to get us out of it as soon as possible.

A few of the men have been oppressed with the heat, and good water is very scarce. This seems to be a very rich soil, made up no doubt of river deposits. A ridge runs parallel with the river, and it is on that elevation all the plantation buildings are located, overlooking the rich country around. The Yazoo River is a very sluggish stream and said to be quite deep. The darkies claim it is "dun full of catfish." I think we may probably have fresh, fish, but not till we *catch* Vicksburg, and then only in case we are allowed to take a rest, for I presume there will then turn up some other stronghold for Grant and his army to take, and for which we shall have to be off as soon as this job is ended. We camped at dark, after a severe and long march, and it is now raining very hard.

May 31st.—We were aroused by the bugle call, and in a few minutes on the march again. Halted at noon on a large plantation. This is a capital place to stop, for the negroes are quite busy baking corn-bread and sweet potatoes for us. We have had a grand dinner at the expense of a rich planter now serving in the southern army. Some of the negroes wanted to come with us, but we persuaded them to remain, telling them they would see hard times if they followed us. They showed indications of good treatment, and I presume their master is one of the few who treat their slaves like human beings.

I must say—whether right or wrong—plantation life has had a sort of fascination for me ever since I came south, especially when I visit one like that where we took dinner today, and some, also, I visited in Tennessee. I know I should treat my slaves well, and, while giving them a good living, I should buy, but never sell.

We left at three o'clock p. m., and just as the boys were ordered to take with them some of the mules working in the field, where there was a large crop being cultivated, to be used, when gathered, for the maintenance of our enemies. As our boys, accordingly, were unhitching the mules, some "dutchy" in an officer's uniform rode up, yelling, "mens! you left dem schackasses alone!" I doubt whether he had authority to give such an order, but whether he had or not he was not obeyed. When we marched off with our corn-bread and "schackasses," some of the darkies insisted on following. We passed through some rebel works at Haines' Bluffs, which were built to protect the approach to Vicksburg by way of the Yazoo River. Sherman had taken

RECEIVING SUPPLIES AT CHICKASAW BAYOU FOR THE ARMY
AROUND VICKSBURG

THE BRIGHT SIDE OF SIEGE LIFE—CAMPING IN THE REAR

NEWSBOYS ARE THICK IN CAMP

them on the nineteenth instant, when our boats came up the river and delivered rations.

May has now passed, with all its hardships and privations to the army of the west—the absence of camp comforts; open fields for dwelling places; the bare ground for beds; cartridge boxes for pillows, and all the other tribulations of an active campaign. Enduring these troubles, we have given our country willing service. We have passed through some hard-fought battles, where many of our comrades fell, now suffering in hospitals or sleeping, perhaps, in unmarked graves. Well they did their part, and much do we miss them. Their noble deeds shall still incite our emulation, that their proud record may not be sullied by any act of ours.

Camped at dark, tired, dirty and ragged—having had no chance to draw clothes for two months.

June 1st.—We stayed in camp all day, much to the enjoyment of the boys. Sergeant Hoover and I got a horse and mule, and rode down to Chickasaw Bayou, where the supplies for our army around Vicksburg are received. I have complained a little of being overmarched, but the trotting of my mule today was the hardest exercise I have had for some time.

If our poor foes in Vicksburg could see our piles of provisions on the river landing, they might hunger for defeat. Around Vicksburg the country is quite hilly and broken, with narrow ridges, between which are deep ravines. These ridges are occupied by the opposing forces at irregular distances. At some points the lines of the Union and Confederate armies are but fifty yards apart.

June 2nd.—We stayed in camp again all day, and I improved the time strolling through the camps, forts and rifle pits, which had been deserted by the Confederates. They seem to have left their quarters rather unceremoniously, for they abandoned siege guns, with tents, wagons, clothing and ammunition scattered about in confusion. I thought, while camped here, they seemed to feel quite secure. They frequently looked towards the Yazoo, and defied our boats to come up. However, when the boats did come, with Sherman in the rear, they beat a hasty retreat to the inside of Vicksburg.

As our duties have been light today, the time has been occupied socially, by the boys reciting many little scenes of the past month. We conversed feelingly of those left behind on account of sickness, or wounds, or death in battle. Only half our company is left now, and after two years more, what will have become of the rest? We shall fight on, perhaps, till the other half is gone. The friendship that now exists among our remnant is very firmly knit. Through our past two years of soldier life such ties of brotherhood have grown up as only companions in arms can know. And I trust before the end of another two years the old flag will again float secure in every State in the Nation.

June 3rd.—Expected to move today, but got orders instead to remain in camp. Have heard heavy cannonading towards Vicksburg, Would prefer to take our place in the line around the city rather than stay away, for there is glory inaction. It may be very nice, occasionally, to rest in camp, but to hear firing and to snuff the battle afar off, creates a natural uneasiness. Besides, if the city should surrender in the meantime, we might be cheated out of our share in a prize, to the taking of which we have contributed some valuable assistance.

Newsboys are thick in camp, with the familiar cries, "*Chicago Times*" and "*Cincinnati Commercial.*" The papers sell quite freely. At home each man wants to buy a paper for himself, but here a single copy does for a whole company, and the one that buys it reads it aloud—a plan which suits the buyer very well, if not the seller. While some of these papers applaud the bravery of the generals and their commands and pray that the brilliancy of past achievements be not dimmed by dissensions in the face of the enemy, other papers have articles that sound to us like treason, slandering the soldier and denouncing the government. But they cannot discourage or demoralise this army, for it was never stronger or more determined than now, and it will continue to strike for our country, even though bleeding at every pore. The rebels cannot be subdued, so they say. Why not? In two years have we not penetrated to the very centre of the South? And in less than that time we shall be seen coming out, covered all over with victory, from the other side.

June 4th,—We move at last. We left camp as the sun rose, reaching our old quarters in front of the rebel Fort Hill in the afternoon. Glad we are to get here. A great change has taken place during our ten days' absence. More rifle-pits have been made and new batteries erected, and our lines generally have been pushed closer to the works of the enemy. Mines are being dug, and we shall soon see something flying in the air in front of us, when those mines explode. The work is being done very secretly, for it would not do to have the rebels find out our plans. Fort Hill in our front and on the Jackson road is said to be the key to Vicksburg. We have tried often to turn this key, but have as often failed. In fact, the lock is not an easy one. The underground work now going on will perhaps break the lock with an explosion. Our return to camp from our excursion after Johnston creates some excitement among those who stayed behind. They all want to hear about our trip, and what we saw and conquered. Our clothes are so dirty and ragged, that though we have sewed and patched, and patched and sewed, Uncle Sam would hardly recognize those nice blue suits he gave us a little while ago. This southern sun pours down a powerful heat, which compels us to keep as quiet as possible. Just a month from today we celebrate our Fourth of July—where, I do not know, but inside of Vicksburg, I hope.

I have asked both officers and men to write in an album I have opened since reaching our old post near the city, and here are a few of their contributions:

Friend O.: Here is hoping we may see the stars and stripes float over the court house in Vicksburg on the Fourth of July, and also that we may see this rebellion, in which so many of our comrades have fallen, come to an end, while we live on to enjoy a peace secured by our arms. Then hurrah for the Buckeye girls. Your sincere friend,

Henry H. Fulton,
Company E, 20th Ohio.

Here is hoping we may have the pleasure of *zweiglass* of lager in Vicksburg, on July 4th.

D. M. Cooper,
Company A, 96th Ohio.

I hope we shall be able to spend the coming Fourth in the famous city before us, and to have a glorification there over our victories.

Squire McKee,
Company E, 20th Ohio.

Here is hoping that by the glorious Fourth, and by the force of our arms, we shall penetrate their boasted Gibraltar.

T. B. Leggett,
Company E, 20th Ohio.

I offer you this toast: Though you have seen many hardships, let me congratulate you on arriving safely so near Vicksburg. May the besieged city fall in time for you and all our boys to take a glass of lager on the Fourth of July; and may the boys of the Twentieth be the first to taste the article they have duly won.

D. B. Linstead,
Company G, 20th Ohio.

June 5th.—The siege is still progressing favourably. There is joy in our camp, for Uncle Sam has again opened a clothing store, which we shall patronize, asking nothing about price or quality. The boys cheered lustily when they saw the teams drive in, and heard what they were loaded with. However, I don't want to hug rifle-pits with a brand new suit on, for it would soon get dirty.

June 6th.—Still banging away. I took a horseback ride around the line to the left in the rear of McClernand's corps. Everywhere I went I was met with the familiar *zip, zip,* of rebel bullets flying promiscuously through the air. I read a northern rebel paper, received by a member of the 96th Ohio, filled with false statements about the soldiers around Vicksburg. It said a great many of Grant's soldiers were deserting. This is of course false, for I have heard of but two deserting their flag in time of need. Those two will never be able to look their old comrades in the face, for if they escape the penalty of death, disgrace and ignominy will not only follow them through life, but stamp their memories and lineage with infamy.

The scorn of every loyal soldier will follow these cowards who have deserted in the face of the foe. No true-hearted mother or father can welcome the return of such recreants, who not only disgrace themselves but all their kindred. This paper also stated that the soldiers around Vicksburg are dying off like flies. This is another falsehood, for the army is in good health and spirits, and looking forward to victory with assurance.

June 7th.—The 20th was at the front all day, sharp shooting. There is a good deal of danger in this kind of business, but we have our fun at it notwithstanding. Another effigy hoisted a little above our rifle-pits, in an instant drew the fire of the enemy. It was our ruse to get them to raise their heads a little, and when they did, we fired back, and the result generally justified the refrain to which our thoughts were moving,

> *Should a rebel show his pate,*
> *To withdraw he'll prove too late.*

We have caught them that way several times.

We still keep unshaken confidence in General Grant, and the ultimate success of our cause. We shall stand firm at our posts, yielding cheerful obedience to all orders, and march bravely on without halting to wrangle and grumble at every imaginary shortcoming in our officers, while our country is in such distress, and when her cries are borne to us upon every breeze. To be in Grant's army, McPherson's corps, Logan's division and the 20th Ohio, commanded by our brave and courteous colonel, M. F. Force, is to be as well off as any soldier in any army in the world.

June 8th.—Another day born in the midst of the rattle of shot and shell. Each day finds us more firmly entrenched amid these hills, until we begin to feel ourselves impregnable.

I visited one of the teeming hospitals to see some boys, and it made me sad enough to look upon some who will soon pass from these scenes of strife. One smooth-cheeked little artillery lad closed his eyes forever, with a last lingering look upon the flag he had hoped to see waving over Vicksburg. His last look was at the flag—his last word was "mother!" Poor boy, when he left home he knew little of the hardships and privations to be endured. War is quite another thing from what my schooldays pictured it. I used to think the two contending armies would march face to face and fire at each other, column by column, but experience has shown me a very different picture, for when the command to fire is given it is often when each man must fire at will, taking shelter where he can, without going too far from his line.

June 9th.—Today our regiment was at the front. The rebels kept pretty quiet; they are learning to behave very well. In fact they might as well lie low and save their powder.

Our men have been employed digging a ditch leading up to Fort Hill, when they intend tunnelling and blowing up the fort. The rebels, however, have got range of the men digging, and have fired upon them. The answering Yankee trick was to shove a car of cotton bales over the trench toward the fort, while the men worked behind it. This served a good purpose for awhile, till the rebs managed to set it on fire; not to be outdone, our boys pushed forward another car well soaked with water. Another Yankee device was contrived—a tower, ten or twelve feet high, with steps inside running to the top, where was hung a looking-glass in such a position as to catch and reflect, to a man inside the tower, the interior of the enemy's fort and rifle pits,

DIGGING A MINE UNDER FORT HILL, WITH A COTTON CAR AS PROTECTION FROM THE ENEMY'S BULLETS.

THE YANKEE LOOKOUT

and thus every man and gun could be counted. This latter contrivance, however, did not last long; it became too conspicuous and dangerous for use.

A report creeps into camp that Johnston is coming with fifty thousand men to raise the siege, but I do not believe it. We have often heard that Richmond had fallen, but it continues within the confederate lines. If the Army of the Potomac does not soon take it. Grant will march us there and seize the prize from; them.

June 10th.—The heat of the sun increases, and we must improve our quarters. Accordingly a part of the day has been spent in cutting cane and building bunks with it on the side of the hill. Such improvements protect us better from the sun.

Last night I sat on the top of a hill while, watching the mortar shells flying into the city from the river. High into the air they leaped, and, like falling stars, dropped, exploding among the houses and shaking even the very hills. The lighted fuse of each shell could be seen as it went up and came down, and occasionally I have seen as many as three of them in the air at once. The fuse is so gauged as to explode the shell within a few feet of the ground. The destruction being thus wrought in the city must be very great. We learn from prisoners that the inhabitants are now living in caves dug out of the sides of the hills. Alas! for the women, children and aged in the city, for they must suffer, indeed, and, should the siege continue several months, many deaths from sickness as well as from our shells, must occur. I am sure Grant has given Pemberton a chance to remove from Vicksburg all who could not be expected to take part in the fearful struggle.

We have been looking for rain to cool the air and lay the dust, and this afternoon we were gratified by a heavy shower.

June 11th.—Stayed in camp today with the exception of about an hour. The rebs have succeeded in planting a mortar, which has sent a few big shells into our quarters. This sort of practice did not last long, for a hundred guns around our line soon roared the mortar to silence. But one shell dropped near my tent, buried itself in the earth, and exploded, scattering dirt for yards around and leaving a hole big enough to bury a horse. Another fell on top of the hill und rolled down, crashing through a tent. The occupants not being at home it failed to find a welcome. These shells are visitors we do not care to see in camp, for their movements are so clumsy they are apt to break things as they go. However, they are rather rare, while the bullets are so frequent that

SHELTERED FROM THE SUN, BUT NOT THE ENEMY'S SHELLS.

A SIBLEY TENT

we have almost ceased to notice them. Their flights remind us of the dropping of leaves and twigs from the trees around us. The balls of lead as they fall are found bent and flattened in every conceivable big shape. A friend from the 96th Ohio, on a visit to me as he walked over, met a rebel bullet which took a piece out of his arm.

June 12th—We expect to be paid off soon, as the pay-rolls are now being made out Money cannot do us much good here among the hills, but we can send it home. Many a family is dependent upon the thirteen dollars a month drawn here by the head of it

When the war is over how many soldiers will be unable to earn, even their own living, to say nothing of that of their families, all on account of wounds or disability incurred in the service, I have heard many a one say he would rather be shot dead in a fight than lose a limb, and thus be compelled to totter through life disabled. But I know our country will be too magnanimous to neglect its brave defenders who have fought its battles till they have become incapacitated for further service. I know we are not fighting for a country that will let its soldiers beg for a living.

We have now but a year left of the term of our enlistment, and the boys are already talking about what they will do. Some say they will stay till peace comes, no matter how long may be the delay, and I think the majority are of this mind. A few, however, will seek their homes when their time runs out, should this war last so long, and the Lord and rebel bullets spare them. For myself, I shall stay, if I can, till the stars and stripes float in triumph once more over all the land. Here are a few lines:

> *To Company E.*
> *You started at your country's call*
> *To tread the fields of blood and strife*
> *Consenting to give up your all—*
> *All, even to your very life.*
> *And many storms of leaden rain*
> *And iron hail have been your lot;*
> *While yet among the number slain*
> *The dear ones North have read you not.*
> *Oh. may you safely yet return*
> *To those who wait your coming, too:*
> *May their fond hearts not vainly yearn*
> *To greet you when the war is through.*

But. though I wish you back in peace,
'Tis not a peace that quite disarms—
'Tis not a full and sure release,
You simply take up other arms.

June 13th.—The siege continues with increased fury, and the boom of cannon announces the sacrifice of more lives. Instead of any cessation the artillery plays upon the city almost every moment throughout the day. The variety of the projectiles becomes greater. The shrapnel, I think, must be most formidable to the enemy. It is a shell filled with eight small balls, which, when the shell is exploded scatter in every direction. It makes a fearful buzzing sound as it flies—a warning to seek cover, if such can be found. Besides this there are the parrot, canister, grape and solid shot. The canister and grape are also cases wherein are enclosed a number of small balls. But the least fragment from an exploded shell is sufficient to wound or kill.

I have a great curiosity to see the court house at Vicksburg. It stands on a hill, and seems to be the target for many cannon. There is a Confederate flag waving from it defiantly. A proud day it will be when we haul it down and raise in its stead the stars and stripes, never to be displaced again. The buildings in the city must, by this time, be pretty well riddled with shot and shell. The women, it seems, did not all leave the city before the bombardment began, and I suppose they have determined to brave it out. Their sacrifices and privations are worthy of a better cause, and were they but on our side how we would worship them. It is rumoured in camp that Grant is getting reinforcements from the eastern army. I have a great desire to see them, for while we have always thought them to be no less brave, they are said to be better clothed and equipped than the western boys.

In fact, from the eastern army, during the last year, the standing report among western boys has been merely such catch phrases as "Bull Run," "Burnside Crossing the Rappahannock," "All Quiet on the Potomac," Perhaps such reports or their substance will continue to fill the headlines of news from those departments until Lincoln commissions Grant commander of the whole army. Should that occur, one grand move forward will be made and the Southern confederacy will be crushed forever.

We are doing all we can to expedite the glorious victory awaiting us here, yet there are grumblers in the North who are complaining of our slow progress, and reasonable articles are published in some papers

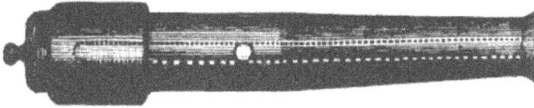

PARROTT RIFLE

PARROTT RIFLE PROJECTILE

SHRAPNEL—

Containing 80 musket balls, fired at Vicksburg. The conception of this missile is due to Lieut.-Gen. Henry Shrapnel, of the English Army. Its velocity is about 1,000 ft. per second.

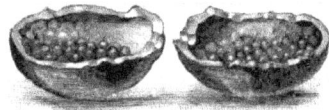

CANISTER SHOT—

is a tin cylinder with iron heads, filled with balls, packed with sawdust. The heads are moveable, and the edges of the tin are turned down over them in place. The balls are made of such a size that seven of them can lie in a bed, one in the middle and six around. These balls are made of cast iron, and are 28 in number.

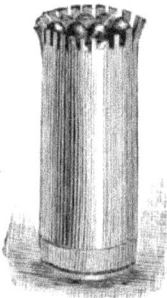

GRAPE SHOT

SOLID SHOT STRAPPED ON A SABOT

that come to us from the North, intended to discourage the soldiers. Why don't Grant move? If we had all those grumblers in Vicksburg, I fancy they would soon find something from Grant was moving quite briskly. But Grant does not idle away his time himself, nor let his men be idle. If the people of the North will but back us up with their aid and confidence, we shall feel well repaid for all the sufferings we endure here, staring death in the face, and standing like a solid wall between their homes and danger.

Let not a murmur meet the ear.
Nor discontent have sway;
Let not a sullen brow appear
Through all the camp today.

June 14th.—Sunday. No bells to ring us to church. I wish we had one day in seven for rest and freedom from care; but there is no such thing now for the soldier. It is shoot, shoot, dodge, dodge, from morning to night, without cessation, except when we are asleep. When the time comes, we can lie down and sleep soundly all night, right under our cannon, firing over us all the time, without disturbing us in the least. But let the long roll be sounded—every man is up at the first tap—for that sound we know means business for us.

Occasionally the rebs plant a mortar in some out of the way spot and drop a shell or two into our midst; but a few well directed shots from our big guns at the rear soon settle them. These rebels obey very well.

We have several large siege guns, lately planted in the rear of our division, which it took ten yoke of oxen to haul, one at a time, to their places. I had been told that the balls from these guns could be seen on their journey, and could not believe it until I put myself in range of the monsters, just behind them, when I found I could see the balls distinctly, as they flew across the hills towards Vicksburg. These guns are nine-inch calibre and they are about twelve feet long. They are monsters, and their voices are very loud.

Sunday is general inspection day, and the officers passed through our quarters at 10 a. m., finding our guns and accoutrements bright and clean. If any young lady at the North needs a good housekeeper, she can easily be accommodated by making a requisition on the 20th Ohio. In fact we can all do patchwork, sew on buttons, make beds and sweep; but I do not think many of us will follow the business after the war is done, for the "relief" always so anxiously looked for by the soldiers must then come.

I heard one of our boys—a high private in the rear rank—lament that he was:

Only a private, and who will care
When I shall pass away?

Poor lad, he was in a sad way! But it was mere homesickness that ailed him. If dissatisfied with his position as a private, let him wait, for if he survives the war, he will, no doubt, have a chance to be captain of an *infant-ry* company.

June 15th.—Our regiment went into the rifle-pits again before daylight, at which time the din of musketry and cannonading from both sides had begun, and will cease only when darkness covers the earth.

We are now so close to Fort Hill that a hard tack was tossed into it by one of our boys, and then held up on a bayonet there, to satisfy us of its safe arrival. Some of the boys have become reckless about the rifle-pits, and are frequently hit by rebel bullets. Familiarity breeds a contempt of danger.

Some of the boys wounded at Raymond have got back to us, and are now ready again to do their part. They are, however, more timid than we who have been at the front so long. It is fun to see these newcomers dodge the balls as they zip along. But they, too, will soon become accustomed to flying lead.

Several of the boys have been hit, but not hurt badly, as the balls were pretty nearly spent before reaching them. Those returning from Raymond say they have marked the graves there, but I fear it will not be long before the last vestige of the resting places of our late comrades will be lost.

June 16th.—We were relieved before daylight, and returned to camp pretty tired. I did not feel well last night, and having had no chance to sleep, I am a little the worse for wear this morning.

There was not much firing done during the night, but we had to keep a good lookout, as there are apprehensions of an outbreak. I do not often go star-gazing, but last night I sat and watched the beauty above. Daytime is glorious, but when night unfurls her banner over care-worn thousands among these hills, and the stars come out from their hiding places, our thoughts seek loftier levels. It was just as though one day had died, and another was born to take its place. Not

JAMES SHELL, BEFORE THE
APPLICATION OF PACKING

JAMES SHELL, AFTER THE
APPLICATION OF PACKING

WHITWORTH PROJECTILE

HAND–GRENADE THROWN
FROM FORT HILL

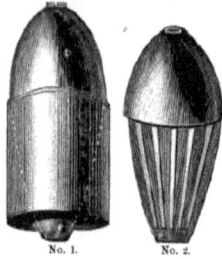

No. 1. No. 2.

SHENKLE'S PROJECTILE.

This projectile, as shown in No. 1, is composed of a cast-iron body. The expanding portion is a papier-mache wad, which being forced on to the cone, is expanded into the rifling of the bore. On issuing from the bore, the wad is blown to pieces, leaving the projectile entirely unincumbered in its flight through the air (No. 2).

SHELL WITH FUSE.—The fuse is graduated on the outside into equal parts, representing seconds and quarter-seconds. In the bottom of this channel is a smooth layer of a composition of lead and tin, with a piece of wick or yarn underneath it. On this is placed a piece of metal. When ready for firing, the dial is gauged at the proper point at which the fuse is to burn through into the shell.

a breeze stirred the foliage, except as fanned by the whirling shells. My thoughts were of home, and of the dear sister there, bedridden, with but little hope of health again. Her dearest wish, I know, is to see her only brother once more before she passes away to that heavenly peace for which she is destined. Through these terrible two years past, thoughts of home and a safe return to an unbroken family circle, have been my constant guiding star.

June 17th.—I was detailed to the charge of a squad of men to guard rebel prisoners in the corral at Logan's headquarters. They were not hard to guard, for they think themselves in pretty good hands, and surely they seem to get better grub here than in their own lines. Some of them are deserters, and upon such I look with contempt. I am ready to share my rations with an honest prisoner, but have no use for a man who enlists in a cause, and then deserts his comrades when they get into a tight place.

If what they say is true, the garrison over there is already familiar with mule meat and scanty meal rations. If they have had to eat mules such as we have killed in the trenches, I pity them, for they are on a tough job. Several cows which I suppose had served families there with milk, we had to kill for browsing too close to our lines.

I am pretty well convinced Pemberton would not hold out much longer but for the help he expects from Johnston, If that, however, is all the hope they have, they might as well surrender at once, for if Johnston should come, he can not do them any good.

A ball struck a little drummer boy a while ago, and he limped off, whimpering: "I wouldn't care a dam, but my other leg has been shot already." Some of the boys went to his assistance, and then they had to hurry towards the hospital, for the rebels got range of them and began firing quite briskly,

I was quite amused to see one of the prisoners brought in today eating his supper. We gave him all he could eat, and that was no small amount. But he was certainly a very hungry man, and if he is a fair sample of those remaining in Vicksburg, Uncle Sam's commissary will have to endure quite a burden, for after the surrender, no doubt, Grant will have to feed them all.

June 18th.—I was relieved from guard at 9 a. m. and returned to camp. There has been very heavy firing all I day, and it is rumoured that Pemberton will try to break through our lines; but if he tries that game he will find it dangerous enough. It is no easy matter to climb

AIMING AT THE COURT HOUSE

A GAME OF EUCHRE, WITH A SHELL FOR TRUMPS

over the bulwark of steel now encircling this city. The weather is getting altogether too hot for comfort. A few sunstrokes have occurred, but without proving fatal so tar. One poor fellow even dropped at midnight, when I presume the surgeon's diagnosis must have been—moonstruck. There are more ways than one of shirking a battle, for which purpose some are even willing to part with a finger or toe.

If the rebels are short of provisions, their ammunition seems to hold out, for they are quite liberal in their distribution of it. But when Sherman begins firing from the east, McClernand from the west, McPherson from the rear, and the mortars from the north, then look out for big fireworks. The cannon are all pointed towards the town, but some of the shells fall far short of it. When these burst in mid-air, we can see a small round cloud of smoke left behind and then there is a sharp lookout for fragments to be scattered in every direction. Our artillerymen have had such good practice during the siege, that they can generally drop a shell wherever they want to.

Boys at the front have time for sport, which is not to be interrupted even by stray shells. I noticed four of our boys playing *euchre*, when a shell from the enemy came careering just above their heads; but they treated it with entire indifference. Another group I saw playing "seven-up" under a blanket caught at the four comers in the hammers of muskets stuck in the ground, and thereby forming a very good shelter from the sun. A shell burst right over this group, scattering its fragments all around, but even this failed to disturb the game, further than to call forth the timely comment, "Johnny passes."

June 19th.—For a month we have been watching our enemy vigilantly, and a panorama, consisting of a great variety of war scenes, has, during that time, passed before us. We have had charging, digging rifle-pits, blowing up forts and firing all sizes of cannon, to say nothing of percussion shells, spherical case shot, time shells, parrot, grape, canister, shrapnel, etc., the memory of which will be vivid to all, both blue and gray, who have seen the show around Vicksburg. The terrible noises, too, that have rung in our ears, must echo for years to come, I may add our endurance to this southern sun, at times being short of rations, and at no time out of danger, yet all the time nearly uncomplaining—everyone trying to make the best of it, and all as merry as the situation would admit.

Each day some of the boys have come in relating new discoveries on reconnoisance, and I do not think there is a foot of ground about

FIGHTING OVER THE ENEMY'S FORTIFICATIONS

these hills that has not been explored, a well or spring that has not been tested, or a single object of interest of any kind that has not been worked till it grew stale. Then each man has had his peculiar view of how a siege like this ought to be conducted—that is, from the standpoint of rank and file. However, we are all agreed that the quiet man in command of our forces is still able to anticipate the requirements of our situation. I call him quiet, for that is just what he is. There is no dash or glitter about him, but he is marked by a steady nerve, and piercing glance that seems to be always on the alert. Many a second lieutenant has fallen a victim to the sharpshooter because of his fresh uniform, while officers of more experience have escaped under slouched hats and old blouses. There seems to be no limit, however, to the experience of some of them.

A cook of the 96th Ohio happened to be cooking beans the other day, when Gen. A. J. Smith, commanding a division of the 13th Army Corps, came around on camp inspection. After being properly saluted by the cook, the general began a colloquy as follows:

Gen, Smith.—What are you cooking?

The Cook.—Beans, sir.

General Smith.—How long do you cook beans?

The Cook.—Four hours, sir.

Gen. Smith (with a look of withering scorn).—*Four hours! You cook 'em six hours!*

That cook's beans were tender enough that day.

Once again the fire of hell
Rained the rebel quarters.
With scream of shot and burst of shell.
And bellowing of the mortars.

June 20th—This morning our whole line of artillery—seven miles long—opened on the doomed city and fortifications at six o'clock, and kept up the firing for four hours, during which time the smoke was so thick we could see nothing but the flash of the guns. No fog could have so completely hid from view objects around, both close and familiar. Had the rebs made a dash for liberty then, they could not have been discovered until they were right upon as. But they did not do it. Our infantry was all called out in line of battle, and we stacked arms till the firing ceased. Oh, what a calm after that terrific bellowing. There was every variety of tone today from the dogs of war— from the squeak of a little fiste to the roar of a bull dog. The sound of some brass pieces was so loud as to drown the reverberations of the larger guns, and not a return shot was fired.

Poor fellows, how tamely they took it! They had nothing to say—at least that we could hear. Several of our boys laid down and slept during the firing as soundly as if they had been on their mothers' feather beds at home. When the clouds cleared away I thought the stars and stripes never looked so beautiful. Even if the defenceless women and children in Vicksburg are protected, or feel as if they were, such a screeching of shot and shell must prove a terror to them, and my heart has not yet grown so hardened that I cannot feel for them.

There is a good deal of complaint, in our company at least, about the coffee we get. It seems not quite so good as that we have had, and I suspect it has been adulterated by somebody who is willing to get rich at the expense of the poor soldier, whose curses will be heaped strong and heavy on anybody who deteriorates any of his rations, and particularly his coffee. The only time a soldier cannot drink his coffee is when the use of that ration is suspended. In fact, there is nothing so refreshing as a cup of hot coffee, and no sooner has a marching column halted, than out from each haversack comes a little paper sack of ground coffee, and a tin cup or tin can, with a wire bale, to be filled from the canteen and set upon a fire to boil. The coffee should not be put in the water before it boils.

At first I was green enough to do so, but soon learned better, being compelled to march before the water boiled, and consequently lost my coffee. I lost both the water and the coffee. It takes but about five minutes to boil a cup of water, and then if you have to march you can put your coffee in and carry it till it is cool enough to sip as you go. Even if we halt a dozen times a day, that many times will a soldier make and drink his coffee, for when the commissary is full and plenty, we may drink coffee and nibble crackers from morning till night. The aroma of the first cup of coffee soon sets the whole 'army to boiling; and the best vessel in which to boil coffee for a soldier is a common cove oyster can, with a bit of bent wire for a bale, by which you can hold it on a stick over the fire, and thus avoid its tipping over by the burning away of its supports.

June 21st.—Today again church bells at the North are calling good people to worship, and to hear words of cheer and comfort to the soul. The prayers of our patriotic mothers and fathers that will go up today for the suppression of this rebellion will surely have a hearing.

DOG OR SHELTER TENT

FRICTION TUBE FOR FIRING CANNON.—
The tube is inserted into the vent of
the cannon and fired by means of a
stout cord, which has a wooden
handle at one end, and an iron hook
at the other: the cannoneer puts
the hook through the loop in the wire
of the friction tube, and holding the
cord by the handle, pulls steadily until the wire is withdrawn, when an
explosion takes place, induced by
the friction of the wire against the
composition in the tube.

COMBINED KNIFE, FORK AND SPOON, USED BY THE BOYS AT
THE SIEGE OF VICKSBURG

We had inspection of arms and quarters at nine this morning. Of course everything was in good order, but if such a thing should take us by surprise some time, our beds might be found not made, and things in general upside down. When notice of this inspection was given, or rather an order to prepare for it, one of our boys remarked, "This must be Sunday;" and he added, "I guess I won't wait for this inspection,—I'll take my girl to church." If his girl had been here the whole company would doubtless have wanted to go to church, too. "Though lost to sight, to memory dear."

We can talk to the sweet creatures only through the dear letters exchanged; but a love letter brings a very bright smile to a warrior's face, and the sunshine that prevails in camp after the reading of the mail from home, is quite noticeable. Dear girls, do not stop writing; write letters that are still longer, for they are the sweetest of war's amenities, and are the only medicine that has kept life in the veins of many a homesick soldier. When the mail comes I cannot help wishing everybody may get a letter; but alas! some must miss hearing their names read, and oh! the sadness that creeps over them when the last name has been called and the last letter handed out to someone else. They are sadder than if wounded by a bullet.

If wounded, a surgeon may prescribe; but what prescription for the failure of a letter from home? Our mail is by no means daily, and if it comes at all, its favours are few and far between. Indeed, each time it comes we get to feeling as if it may never come again. And so it may prove, in fact. The disappointed one carries his strangled hope into the next day's fight, falls, and dies, perhaps, from some wound that otherwise might prove slight, for his heart is broken.

This afternoon I stood on a little hill just back of a regiment adjoining, talking with a friend there, when crash through his brain went a rebel bullet. He had just alluded to the horrors of the daily strife. Relieved from further duty here, he went to answer roll-call in a better army, to which his honourable discharge from this ought surely to admit him. He answered the first call of his country, and had served faithfully through two years of hardship and danger. I personally know that he fought well, and his name should not fail to be enrolled somewhere in the records of his country.

June 22nd.—Johnston is getting lively again, and beginning to kick up a dust in the rear; so we have orders to move tonight, with three days' cooked rations. One regiment from each brigade in Logan's division constitute our expedition, which, I think, will find him, and if we get sight of his army, somebody will be likely to get hurt.

It is now just a month since we made the charge on the enemy's line which proved to us so disastrous, and our cannon now are too close to act on Fort Hill, so a wooden gun has been made, which, charged with a small amount of powder, throws the shell inside the fort—a new device, but working well, for it can drop its missile where the cannon cannot.

We have eaten pretty well in camp today, and cooked everything we had on hand, since we may not get so good an opportunity again upon the march. When hard tack was first issued there was but one way to eat it, and that was dry, just as it reached us. Practice, however, taught us to prepare a variety of dishes from it. The most palatable way to dispose of hard tack, to my taste, is to pulverize, then soak overnight, and fry for breakfast as batter-cakes. Another good way is to soak whole, and then fry; and still another is to soak a little, then lay it by the fire and let grease drop on it from toasted meat, held to the fire on a pointed stick. This latter is the most common way on a march. Sometimes the tack is very hard indeed by the time it reaches us, and it requires some knack to break it.

I have frequently seen boys break it over their knees. Just raise your foot up so as to bring the bent knee handy, and then fetch your hard tack down on it with your right hand, with all the force you can spare, and, if not too tough, you may break it in two. But one poor fellow I saw was completely exhausted trying to break a hard tack, and after resorting to all the devices he could think of, finally accomplished it by dropping on it a 12-pound shell. The objection to that plan was, however, that the fellow could hardly find his hard tack afterward.

At midnight we crept out of camp unobserved—everything being quiet except now and then a shot on picket line.

June 23rd.—We halted this morning at six o'clock, and but a few minutes elapsed before two-thirds of the regiment were fast asleep. A few very hungry ones, only, made coffee and took breakfast.

We find ourselves again on the road to Jackson, but what our final destination is, no one knows except the *stars* in front. We surmise our course to be through Johnston's army, if we can find it.

The "blarsted" bugle blasted us out on the road again at seven. I believe I, for one, would rather have spent my hour m eating than sleeping. However, we trudged our eight miles at an easy pace and halted again. The birds were singing merrily, with no sounds of war to interfere. It is rumoured that we are out hunting the paymaster instead of Johnston.

June 24th.—Awaiting orders to march is as tiresome as waiting at a station for a train. We were ready for marching orders again this morning, but failed to get them.

The weather is hot. Some of the rebel prisoners have said we could not stand this heat, but I guess the Yanks can stand it if they can, and if it should actually get too hot, we will just cool their country off. The nights are pleasant enough and we are thankful for the comfort of the sleep which they allow us. We have a chance out here to forage a little, and though but little, any change from array rations becomes agreeable.

It is amazing what progress soldiers make in foraging. They began committing such depredations as to cause an order on the subject to be issued, and on the eighth of May last the commanding general required a general order, prohibiting foraging, to be read throughout the army five times a day. Not long after that, two soldiers of the 13th corps were arrested and brought before General A. J. Smith, at his headquarters in a fine grove of stately poplars, where the general was informed by the guard that the men had been caught in the act of stealing chickens. The gallant general appeared to be revolving the heinousness of the chaise as he looked aloft among the poplars, and presently the guard inquired what should be done with the men, when the general, after another glance upward, turning to the guard, replied, "Oh, damn 'em, let 'em go. There ain't any tree here high enough to hang 'em on."

June 25th.—We have orders to stay in camp, ready to move at a moment's notice. Our marching orders are still delayed, so we have enjoyed a good rest. We are now out of hearing of the guns at Vicksburg, and it seems very still around us, indeed.

The term of the enlistment of some members of our regiment has now expired, and they seem to want to get home again to see their mamas: but go they cannot until our "rabbit is caught." Shame on them for wanting to leave before the flag flies over Vicksburg. Many of them have had letters from friends at the North, urging them not to stay after their time is out. But they may as well make up their minds that Grant will hold them till Vicksburg is taken.

June 26th.—We have heard that Port Hudson is ours, and I hope this may be true, for it will tend to hasten the surrender of Vicksburg.

A little dirt has been thrown up ahead of us, as a shield, in case we have to fight the enemy. We hear all sorts of reports about the strength of Johnston's army, but the truth will only appear when we meet it. One captive said the report in Vicksburg was that Pemberton despaired of getting help from the outside, and was ready to surrender when the last meal rations have been eaten He probably understands the resources of our commissary, as well as the magnanimous disposition of Grant to issue provisions to a starving foe. Well; why not? The first square meal received from Uncle Sam will be an occasion to them of thanksgiving. They will get the best that we can issue. And when the war is over, true soldiers of both armies will be among the first to break the bread of reunion and quaff the cup of restored peace and good will.

June 27th.—A number of our boys went a few miles, blackberrying, and picked quite a quantity to bring home, when we heard the sound of horses' hoofs, and suddenly concluding we had berries enough, we beat a hasty retreat for camp and got there safely.

The weather is not quite as hot here as it Was in our close quarters at the front, but while we enjoy that change we would much prefer remaining at our post there, until the end of the siege.

Some of the boys have had to boil their pants—the only process which is sure death to an enemy lurking there which we find most troublesome. While our pants are boiling the owner leans over the kettle anxiously, for it is probably his only pair. Well, it is now summer time, and, it will do to sun ourselves an hour or two. These little pests lurking in our pants become very annoying when they go foraging. These creatures are about the only war relics from which I have not gathered specimens to send home. I have, in fact, *gathered* enough of them, but with no view to a museum or cabinet.

It is fun to see a fellow get into a pair of boiled pants. The boiling has shrunk them till they fail to reach the top of his brogans by some inches, and accordingly he bends over to try to pull them down to a junction, when the contrary things seem to recoil still further; and the only satisfaction left to him at last—and it is no mean one, either—is that they are at least clean, and he himself is once more their sole occupant, How long he will remain so, however, it is hard to say.

June 28th.—The boys of the 20th left at Vicksburg joined our regiment today. We were very anxious to hear how the siege was progressing, and, to our surprise, learned that it was going right on as usual, without our assistance. It was interesting to hear of the blowing up of Fort Hill by our division, but we did not ascertain the number killed, though the explosion

> *Hoisted two or three.*
> *And blew a darky free*
> *From slavery to freedom.*

This negro, blown up with other chattels in the fort, was dropped into our lines and taken to General Logan's headquarters, none the worse for his trip. When asked what he saw, he said, "As I was comin' down I met massa gwine up." Nothing, however, was gained by blowing up the fort, except planting the stars and stripes thereon, by our troops who made the charge after the explosion; but our colours were removed, for safety, after dark. While our men lay all the afternoon on the side of the fort, the rebels threw into their ranks hand-grenades which killed and wounded quite a number. Our boys, however, would occasionally catch them and toss them back to the place from which they came, just in time to explode among their owners.

Living out here in the woods is quite different from camping before Vicksburg. Yet all is life and bustle wherever we are, from reveille at daybreak, to tattoo at night. Each man must answer to his name in ranks at roll-call in the morning, and must be properly dressed. Some of the most ludicrous scenes of army life are to be witnessed at this exercise. A few of the old fashioned, steady fellows, as a general thing appear quite thoroughly dressed; but as you go down the ranks from the head where they stand, you will begin to find, now and then, a man who has but one boot or shoe on, with the other but half way on. Another boy will be putting on his blouse—having grabbed it in the dark—of course wrong side out. Another has tossed his blouse over his shoulders, and is trying to hide close to his right-hand man. Still another, trying to get his pants on between his bed and the line, has caught a foot in the lining, and hops along like a sore-footed chicken.

I saw one fellow come out, at the foot of the company, wrapped only in a blanket. The orderly, however, sent him back to be better uniformed; he could not play Indian at morning roll-call. The last one of those who have overslept, makes his appearance holding on to his clothes with both hands. Some answer to their names before taking position in the ranks, and in fact, even some before they are

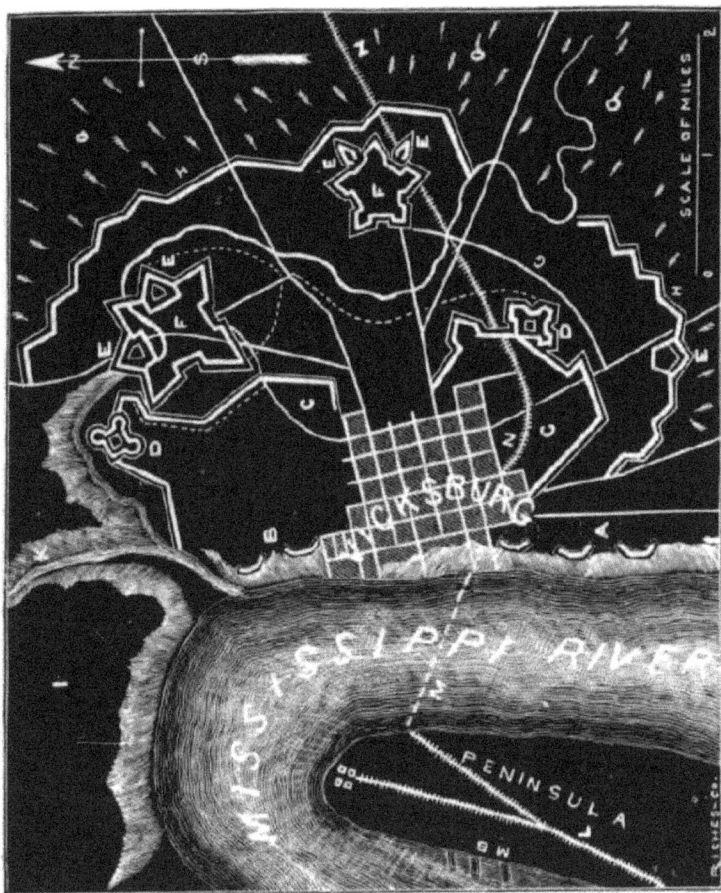

EXPLANATIONS.

A. Lower Water Batteries.
B. Upper Water Batteries.
C. Inner Lines of Defense.
D. Redoubt. (A Fortification breast high.)
E. Redan. (A Fortification in the shape of the letter A.)
F. Fort.
G. Road.
Dotted Lines. Rifle Pits.

H. Outer Lines of Defense.
I. Walnut Bluffs.
K. Bayou.
L. Shreveport Railroad.
M. Ferry.
M. B. Mortar Boats.
N. Jackson Railroad.
O. Abattis. (Trees or branches of Trees to impede the approach of Assailants.)

fairly out of bed. A company which has for its orderly a person who is a little lenient, fares well; but if he is inclined to strain his authority, he is bound to have its ill-will. After roll-call, some of the half-dressed return to bed for another snooze, while the rest complete their toilet. After that comes the splitting of rails, building of fires, and a general rash for breakfast, which winds up the duties of the morning.

June 29th.—The 4th of July is fast approaching, and if we do not get our prize by that time, we will have a little celebration out here in the woods, for we have flags, drums and plenty of spread-eagle speakers, and we can omit the cannon, of which kind of music we have had a surfeit. Yes, we have all the material for a patriotic celebration, but I had hoped we should waive the old flag in Vicksburg that day.

I was sick last night, and up many times before day; and as I walked among the sleepers, I was astonished at the snoring; the variety of sounds made was as great as that of a brass band.

A rumour circulates that Pemberton has made an attack on our lines at Vicksburg, trying to cut his way out, but failed of his purpose. From a prisoner brought in, I have learned, by questioning, that the rebel authorities have made numerous drafts for young and old, to re-fill their ranks, and I think their army now must be as strong as it can ever be. By conscription and terrorism they have forced into the field every available man. With the North it is not so, for the old song, "*We are Coming, Father Abraham, Three Hundred Thousand More,*" is being sung there yet, with goodwill, and volunteers are still pouring in to fill up what may be lacking in our ranks. We can thus throw renewed forces against failing ones.

June 30th.—Our dreams were broken this morning at daylight by the bugle call, and in a very few minutes the whole command was up and ready to march—their beds around the owners' necks. Our woollen blankets are rolled up as tight as possible, having a rubber one outside, which, when the two ends are tied, are swung around our necks. If there has been a rain to wet the blankets, and no time to dry them, they make a heavy load on the march; so no time is lost in drying blankets whenever the opportunity is offered. If it is raining when we retire, and brush can be cut to lay the blankets on, we get a number one spring bed, and when the weather is pleasant a good bed can be made by laying down two rails the width of the blanket apart, and filling the space with grass, or straw from any adjacent stack, on which the blankets may be spread.

THE CHARGE AND REPULSE AT FORT HILL

There is a sort of tall grass growing in this country which makes a soft bed, and is quite worth the pulling. Everything possible is done by the soldier to secure a good night's sleep. I have seen straw stacks torn to pieces, sheds pulled down, and fences melt away in the twinkling of an eye, about camp time. A certain officer has ordered his men to take only the top rail, which order was obeyed to the letter, yet every rail disappeared—the bottom rail finally becoming the top one. I have seen half a regiment bearing rails, boards and straw toward camp before even the end of the day's march was reached. They will have good beds and fires.

July 1st.—Here we enter upon the patriotic month of July, and where and how we are to spend it is yet beyond our conjecture, for we never know in this kind of service what a day may bring forth.

Preparations appear to have been made here for remaining in camp, and yet we may sleep tonight many miles away, or perhaps, without sleeping, march the whole night through. If only life is spared, it is enough; our duties are not shirked. If we camp only for a day, our quarters are to be all cleaned up, and everything put in the beat order possible for comfort. On such excursions as this we have no mess cooking, but every fellow cooks for himself. The first man up in the morning, therefore, gets the frying-pan, from whom the next must engage it, and then may come number three, who is referred to number two. So the utensil goes round a group or mess. The coffee is generally made in a camp kettle for the entire company. I have spent more time hunting up the owner of the last claim on the frying- pan than it afterward took to fry my bacon and crackers.

The paymaster is said to be not far from camp, which creates quite an excitement, since he may charge upon us any moment. There were orders for inspection every morning at eight o'clock for all companies. A little exercise of this kind hurts nobody. I took a stroll through the woods, looking at the graves of those who had fallen by the way-side while our army fought for the position it now holds around Vicksburg. These graves will soon be levelled, and their last trace lost. Friends may mourn for the fallen, but their tears will never water the graves of the heroes.

I write with the aid of a bayonet candle-stick. The latter end of this month will find me just twenty-one years of age.

July 2nd.—This is Camp Tiffin. Our regiment was favoured to-day with a large mail, and nothing could have been more acceptable.

This is a fac-simile of a "hard-tack", issued to the author at Vicksburg. The scene upon it represents a soldier toasting his cracker, and the spots in the cracker were caused by the worms which inhabited it.

Letters from home were looked into first, and next, of course, came sweethearts. One letter was read aloud, describing the capture of a butternut camp, in Holmes County, Ohio. The fort was built on a hill, and manned with several cannon, to resist the draft. A few soldiers from Camp Chase, however, went over and soon put an end to that attempt at resistance. I regret to hear of such a disgraceful affair occurring in my native State. From other letters and papers it appears this thing occurs in many other Northern States, and of course it must give encouragement to the rebels.

The rumour now runs that the paymaster will be at hand tomorrow, but he is about as reliable as Johnston, for we have been something like a week looking for both these gentlemen. I confess I would rather meet greenbacks than graybacks.

This afternoon, with several others, I went blackberrying again, and in searching for something to eat, we paid a visit to a house where, to our happy surprise, we found a birthday party, brightened by the presence of no less than eleven young ladies. We asked, of course, where "the boys" were, and they replied, as we expected, "out hunting Yanks." Well, we found it a treat to get a taste of sociality once more, after being so long famished. They were very nice rebel girls, though I think the colour of the eyes of one of them was what I might call *true blue*. They asked us to lunch with them, which we did with pleasure. The eatables were good, and we had a splendid time—all the while, of course, keeping one eye on the girls and the other on the window. We told our experience at our last blackberrying excursion, when they assured as we had nothing to fear with them, for they were all "for the Union." No doubt they will be whenever their "boys" come home.

July 3rd.—Uncle Sam's cashier has arrived at last, and we have been paid for two months' service. The married men are quite anxious to send their money home to their wives and little ones. It is risky sending money North from here, yet, to some, more dangerous to keep it. I saw two boys sitting on a log, today, playing poker at five cents a game. Five cent currency is paid in a sheet, and, as either lost the game, a five cent piece was torn off.

THE FOURTH OF JULY! The siege is at last ended. Behold the white flag now waving over the rebel ramparts. Vicksburg has at length surrendered. Speed the glad news to our loved ones at the North, who, during our long trial, have helped us with their prayers. Speed it to the entire forces of the Union, that they may all take courage. and move again.

We are all full of rejoicing, as the event will no doubt prove a death-blow to the rebellion m the Southwest. Vicksburg has been the boast of the enemy, who thought it to be impregnable, and they confidently defied the Army of the West to take it. But by the untiring energy, skill and forecast of our gallant leader, U. S. Grant, aided by the willing and brave hearts about him, Vicksburg has been taken, and over it the stars and stripes now float proudly in all their majestic beauty. How glad I am that I have been one of those who have endured the trials requisite to plant our banner there.

And while rejoicing over our success, let us not forget those who have died on these fields of honour. While we surviving raise Liberty's ensign over Vicksburg, let us remember the graves at Raymond and Champion Hills, And in after years, when we meet to refresh the memory of soldier days, let our dead here around Vicksburg never be forgotten. Let us think of them as standing guard over our dearly-won prize, until the final roll-call, when each shall be "present" or "accounted for."

They struggled and fell, their life-blood staining
The assaulting foeman's hand;
And clasping freedom's flag, sustaining.
Cried, God save our native land.
Let angels spread their wings protecting;
Let sweetest flowers ever bloom;
And let green bays, our faith reflecting,
Mark each martyr's sacred tomb.

Now that the enemy have resigned possession of Vicksburg, I trust the wicked rebellion will not fail soon to near its end, when all our boys in blue will have leave, at will, *to present arms* to the girls they left behind them. A star heralding the coming peace already seems to twinkle in the sky. We rejoice not less over our triumph today because it was consummated upon the glorious Fourth. And while we rejoice for our country, we show no unworthy exultation over the fallen, to whom we extend the sympathy of victors.

Our division, under its commander. General Logan, marched into the city in triumph, and there took command and completed the long desired event—raising the star spangled banner over the court house cupola.

The armies of the Union
Round Vicksburg long had lain;
For forty-seven days and nights
Besieging it in vain.

Then came the morning of the Fourth.
Our Nation's jubilee—
Ah, could the news this hour go north—
In Vicksburg soon we'll be.

The siege is done, the struggle past
On this eventful day
Glad triumph crowns us. as, at last.
Our thanks to God we pay.

Above the vanquished walls I stand.
My country, proud to see
The festive hosts, with flag and band.
Parading gloriously.

O, glorious Fourth! O blissful day!
How hearts of thousands swell
To see such toils such hopes repay.
Such dangers end so well."

LEONAUR

ALSO FROM LEONAUR
AVAILABLE IN SOFTCOVER OR HARDCOVER WITH DUST JACKET

THE WOMAN IN BATTLE *by Loreta Janeta Velazquez*—Soldier, Spy and Secret Service Agent for the Confederacy During the American Civil War.

BOOTS AND SADDLES *by Elizabeth B. Custer*—The experiences of General Custer's Wife on the Western Plains.

FANNIE BEERS' CIVIL WAR *by Fannie A. Beers*—A Confederate Lady's Experiences of Nursing During the Campaigns & Battles of the American Civil War.

LADY SALE'S AFGHANISTAN *by Florentia Sale*—An Indomitable Victorian Lady's Account of the Retreat from Kabul During the First Afghan War.

THE TWO WARS OF MRS DUBERLY *by Frances Isabella Duberly*—An Intrepid Victorian Lady's Experience of the Crimea and Indian Mutiny.

THE REBELLIOUS DUCHESS *by Paul F. S. Dermoncourt*—The Adventures of the Duchess of Berri and Her Attempt to Overthrow French Monarchy.

LADIES OF WATERLOO *by Charlotte A. Eaton, Magdalene de Lancey & Juana Smith*—The Experiences of Three Women During the Campaign of 1815: Waterloo Days by Charlotte A. Eaton, A Week at Waterloo by Magdalene de Lancey & Juana's Story by Juana Smith.

NURSE AND SPY IN THE UNION ARMY *by Sarah Emma Evelyn Edmonds*—During the American Civil War

WIFE NO. 19 *by Ann Eliza Young*—The Life & Ordeals of a Mormon Woman During the 19th Century

DIARY OF A NURSE IN SOUTH AFRICA *by Alice Bron*—With the Dutch-Belgian Red Cross During the Boer War

MARIE ANTOINETTE AND THE DOWNFALL OF ROYALTY *by Imbert de Saint-Amand*—The Queen of France and the French Revolution

THE MEMSAHIB & THE MUTINY *by R. M. Coopland*—An English lady's ordeals in Gwalior and Agra during the Indian Mutiny 1857

MY CAPTIVITY AMONG THE SIOUX INDIANS *by Fanny Kelly*—The ordeal of a pioneer woman crossing the Western Plains in 1864

WITH MAXIMILIAN IN MEXICO *by Sara Yorke Stevenson*—A Lady's experience of the French Adventure

LEONAUR

ALSO FROM LEONAUR
AVAILABLE IN SOFTCOVER OR HARDCOVER WITH DUST JACKET

A DIARY FROM DIXIE *by Mary Boykin Chesnut*—A Lady's Account of the Confederacy During the American Civil War

FOLLOWING THE DRUM *by Teresa Griffin Vielé*—A U. S. Infantry Officer's Wife on the Texas frontier in the Early 1850's

FOLLOWING THE GUIDON *by Elizabeth B. Custer*—The Experiences of General Custer's Wife with the U. S. 7th Cavalry.

LADIES OF LUCKNOW *by G. Harris & Adelaide Case*—The Experiences of Two British Women During the Indian Mutiny 1857. A Lady's Diary of the Siege of Lucknow by G. Harris, Day by Day at Lucknow by Adelaide Case

MARIE-LOUISE AND THE INVASION OF 1814 *by Imbert de Saint-Amand*—The Empress and the Fall of the First Empire

SAPPER DOROTHY *by Dorothy Lawrence*—The only English Woman Soldier in the Royal Engineers 51st Division, 79th Tunnelling Co. during the First World War

ARMY LETTERS FROM AN OFFICER'S WIFE 1871-1888 *by Frances M. A. Roe*—Experiences On the Western Frontier With the United States Army

NAPOLEON'S LETTERS TO JOSEPHINE *by Henry Foljambe Hall*—Correspondence of War, Politics, Family and Love 1796-1814

MEMOIRS OF SARAH DUCHESS OF MARLBOROUGH, AND OF THE COURT OF QUEEN ANNE VOLUME 1 by A. T. Thomson

MEMOIRS OF SARAH DUCHESS OF MARLBOROUGH, AND OF THE COURT OF QUEEN ANNE VOLUME 2 by A. T. Thomson

MARY PORTER GAMEWELL AND THE SIEGE OF PEKING *by A. H. Tuttle*—An American Lady's Experiences of the Boxer Uprising, China 1900

VANISHING ARIZONA *by Martha Summerhayes*—A young wife of an officer of the U.S. 8th Infantry in Apacheria during the 1870's

THE RIFLEMAN'S WIFE *by Mrs. Fitz Maurice*—*The Experiences of an Officer's Wife and Chronicles of the Old 95th During the Napoleonic Wars*

THE OATMAN GIRLS *by Royal B. Stratton*—The Capture & Captivity of Two Young American Women in the 1850's by the Apache Indians

www.ingramcontent.com/pod-product-compliance
Lightning Source LLC
Chambersburg PA
CBHW021059090426
42738CB00006B/419